COMPLETE EDITION
ACOUSTIC
BLUES GUITAR

Beginning • Intermediate • Mastering

LOU MANZI

Stream or download the audio content for this book.
To access, visit: **alfred.com/redeem**
Enter the following code: 00-36422_445544

CONTENTS

Alfred Music
P.O. Box 10003
Van Nuys, CA 91410-0003
alfred.com

ISBN-10: 0-7390-7400-8 (Book & Online Audio)
ISBN-13: 978-0-7390-7400-8 (Book & Online Audio)

Cover photo © David Redfern / Redferns

BEGINNING ACOUSTIC

BLUES GUITAR

Audio tracks recorded and engineered by Collin Tilton at Bar None Studio, Northford, CT
The guitar used on the recording and in all photos of the author was made by Thomas Bazzolo
www.bazzolo.com

ABOUT THE AUTHOR

PHOTO BY TIMOTHY PHELPS

Lou Manzi has been performing his original and dynamic style of acoustic blues since the 1970s. He has written four fingerstyle guitar books, including *Beginning Fingerstyle Guitar* (Alfred Music #14099). Lou has performed extensively as a solo artist and with Rob Fletcher as half of the Fletcher & Manzi duo. Their CD, *Horsin' Around Live,* features original songs that are a blend of blues, jazz and rock. He also appears on *Remembrance,* a compilation CD that is a tribute to American veterans.

Lou is a guitar instructor at several Connecticut schools and has taught at the National Guitar Workshop since 1984. Recognized as a prominent teacher of the acoustic guitar and the blues, he has conducted seminars throughout the United States.

DEDICATION
The Complete Acoustic Blues Guitar Method is dedicated to my parents. I saw the Beatles. I wanted a guitar. They bought one for me. One gift among millions of others.

And to the memory of Dave Van Ronk who passed away in 2002. As a true original and a very special performer, he was a giant influence on countless musicians. Listen to his music—you'll hear the sound of a man who put his heart and soul into every note he sang and played.

ACKNOWLEDGEMENTS
Thanks to Ronnie Earl whose music showed me how strong and deep the blues can be; to Nat and the staffs of Workshop Arts and Alfred for the opportunity to share with others my love of the music; to Dave, Barbara, Paula and all my friends at the National Guitar Workshop, for all they've given me over the years; and to Rob Fletcher for all the fun and inspiration.

TABLE OF CONTENTS

00

Track 1

Online audio is included with this book to make learning easier and more enjoyable. The symbol shown on the left appears next to every example in the book that features an audio track. Use the recordings to ensure you're capturing the feel of the examples and interpreting the rhythms correctly. The track number below the symbol corresponds directly to the example you want to hear (example numbers are above the icon). All the track numbers are unique to each "book" within this volume, meaning every book has its own Track 1, Track 2, and so on. (For example, *Beginning Acoustic Blues Guitar* starts with Track 1, as does *Intermediate Acoustic Blues Guitar* and *Mastering Acoustic Blues Guitar*.) Track 1 for each book will help you tune your guitar.

See page 1 for instructions on how to access the online audio.

ABOUT THIS BOOK

Welcome to *The Complete Acoustic Blues Guitar Method,* a comprehensive series of books designed specifically for the aspiring acoustic blues guitarist. This method consists of three separate volumes now available in this complete edition. Each of the three volumes (*Beginning Acoustic Blues Guitar, Intermediate Acoustic Blues Guitar* and *Mastering Acoustic Blues Guitar*) is an important step along the way to mastering the acoustic blues guitar.

You've made a great choice in learning to play the blues—and what better instrument to play them on than the acoustic guitar, which has been a beloved sidekick to blues players since the earliest days of the style. If you're a true beginner, you'll find the first steps in this book easy and fun. There is also a lot to offer the more experienced player. Either way, you're sure to find the blues a rich and rewarding style to play.

With a little practice, most of the musical examples in this book will be easy to master. The music on the recording will probably sound familiar to you; many great blues artists use the techniques in this book. Make it your goal to learn all of the music in each chapter and you'll be well on your way to becoming a real blues player.

You don't have to go through the book page by page. You may find it more fun to jump around. Play the easier examples first and, as you improve, begin to work on more difficult material. Another option is to listen to the recording and tackle your favorite examples or songs first. Make sure, however, to learn the music theory that is covered; it will make you a better player.

The blues has deeply influenced rock, jazz, country, R&B and almost every other style of music. As a blues player, you will be familiar with many elements found in these other styles and have a good head start when learning any contemporary music.

The blues is like a well. You can scoop some water from the surface and get a refreshing drink. This would be like a person taking their first steps, learning a few songs. But the well is *deep,* and there's *good* water all the way to the bottom. You can play the blues for years and continue to learn and drink from this well. Your mastery of the material in this book is just your first drink. Enjoy!

CHAPTER 1

Getting Started

CHOOSING STRINGS

Walk into any well stocked music store and you will see the inevitable "Wall of Strings." Choosing a set of strings for your guitar can be confusing for a beginner.

How often you need to change your strings depends on how much you play and your personal taste. Newer strings will always sound brighter than older ones. Older strings lose their tone, do not stay in tune as well and may even start to rust. Don't let your strings get to that point. You should change them when they start to lose their brilliance.

To play acoustically, you need *acoustic guitar strings*. The 3rd, 4th, 5th and 6th strings are thin steel cores wound in thin bronze.

Strings come in different thicknesses or *gauges*. Most of the sets you'll see in stores are *extra light, light* and *medium* gauge. Try different gauges now and then to see which you prefer for your guitar. As a rule, the thicker the string, the richer the tone. However, there is a disadvantage to using thicker strings. They are more difficult to play. The thicker the string, the more effort is needed to press the strings against the frets. Keep in mind that certain chords are much easier to play with thinner strings. Another reason to use light gauge strings is that you'll be learning how to *bend* strings. This requires you to push or pull a string either up or down. This is easier to accomplish with lighter strings.

You can also use *custom light* gauge strings, which are somewhere between light and extra light. The sound is good and they are easy to play, which is very important if you play a lot. It is important to keep your hands in good health.

THE OPEN STRINGS

The thinnest string, the one closest to the floor, is the *1st string*. The others are numbered consecutively to the thickest string, the *6th string*, which is closest to the ceiling. It will be helpful to memorize the names of the strings (included in the chart below) as soon as possible. The sentence, "**E**rnie's **A**nt **D**oes **G**et **B**ig **E**ventually," can help you in this process.

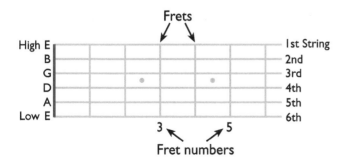

TUNING

You can tune by matching your strings to the tuning notes on Track I of the recording for this book. Here are two other ways you can tune your guitar.

ELECTRONIC TUNER

The best way for a beginner to tune is to use an *electronic tuner*. Not only is this the quickest, easiest and most reliable way, it also accustoms the beginner's musical "ear" to how the strings are supposed to sound. Most professional players use electronic tuners because of their speed and accuracy—and because they allow performers to tune quietly (which is very useful during a performance).

There are two types of tuners: *guitar tuners* and *chromatic tuners*. A guitar tuner is designed to tune the strings in *standard tuning*: E–A–D–G–B–E. A chromatic tuner allows you to tune a string to any *pitch* (degree of highness or lowness of a *tone* or musical sound). This is helpful when using *alternate tunings,* which are any tunings *other* than standard tuning.

RELATIVE TUNING

It is also vitally important that you learn to tune without an electronic tuner. You can do this using *relative tuning,* where the strings are tuned by comparing their pitches to one another.

To use this method, you need a *reference tone.* You can get this from a tuning fork, a pitch pipe, a piano or another guitar. A good pitch to start with is E (12 white keys below middle C on the piano), to which you would match your 6th string. If you do not have a reference pitch to start with, approximate it the best you can. As long as all the strings are tuned in relation to each other, your guitar will sound in tune.

1.   Match the open 6th string (low E—the string closest to your chin when the guitar is placed in proper playing position, see page 18) to your reference tone (E).

2.   Match the open 5th string to the A on the 5th fret of the 6th string.

3.   Match the open 4th string to the D on the 5th fret of the 5th string.

4.   Match the open 3rd string to the G on the 5th fret of the 4th string.

5.   Match the open 2nd string to the B on the 4th fret of the 3rd string.

6.   Match the open 1st string to the E on the 5th fret of the 2nd string.

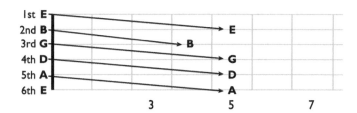

Track I

You can also tune to Track I of the recording.

MUSICAL PITCHES AND THE FRETBOARD

HALF STEPS AND WHOLE STEPS

A *half step* is the distance of one fret on the guitar. For example, press any string at any fret. Now go one fret higher (closer to the body of the guitar). The distance between those two pitches is a half step.

A *whole step* is the distance of two frets on the guitar, or two half steps. Once again, press any string at any fret. Now go two frets higher (skip one fret). The distance between those two pitches is a whole step.

From any open string to the 1st fret is the distance of a half step. From any open string to the 2nd fret is a whole step.

THE MUSICAL ALPHABET

The *musical alphabet* consists of seven letters that repeat: A–B–C–D–E–F–G, A–B–C, etc. Each of these letters represents a musical pitch. These seven pitches are the *natural* pitches. On a piano, they are the white keys.

Only two sets of natural pitches are a half step apart: E–F and B–C.

ACCIDENTALS

The pitches between the natural pitches are *accidentals*. The symbols used to represent them are:

♯   *Sharp.* Raises a pitch one half step (one fret).

♭   *Flat.* Lowers a pitch one half step (one fret).

♮   *Natural.* Returns a pitch to its natural position.

These raised and lowered pitches are the black keys on a piano.

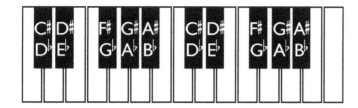

Notice that each black key, or pitch between the natural pitches, has two names. Each of these can be viewed as a raised tone (when moving a half step up from a white key) or a lowered tone (when moving a half step down from a white key). Because of this, they can be called by a sharp name or a flat name (depending on the musical situation). For example, the first black key in the illustration above can be called C♯ or D♭ . The two names given to the same pitch are called *enharmonic equivalents*.

When combined, the natural pitches and accidentals make up the 12 pitches used to play music. Notice that the letters repeat themselves in the illustration below. This is because the pitch-names repeat every 12 half steps. The distance of 12 half steps between two pitches with the same name is an *octave*. Because an instrument usually spans several octaves, there are many more tone choices than the 12 actual pitch-names.

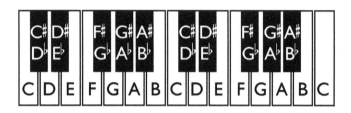

THE GUITAR FRETBOARD

On the guitar we don't have the visual aid of black and white keys; all the frets look the same. However, the same chromatic (half-step) principle makes it easy for us to name every note on the guitar. The following chart gives the names of the pitches on each string—from the open strings to the 17th fret.

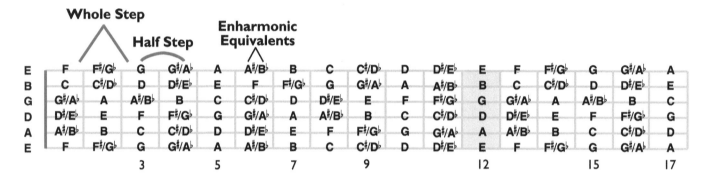

If you start with any open string and go 12 half steps (12 frets) up (toward the body), you will have gone the distance of an octave and played every pitch-name there is. Notice also, you will have arrived at the letter with which you started. E is the open 1st string; if you go to the 12th fret, you arrive again at E. This is the same for all the strings and for every pitch.

Learn the fretboard

1. Start by memorizing the string names (if you haven't already).

2. Then apply the musical alphabet, keeping in mind the two sets of natural pitches that are a half step apart (E–F, B–C).

3. Go string by string. First, name all the natural pitches. Then, using accidentals, name ALL the pitches.

Learning the fretboard is essential for a guitarist. Not only will it prove useful throughout this book, but also throughout your experience as a guitar player.

STANDARD MUSIC NOTATION

To get the most out of this book (and future studies), a functional knowledge of *standard music notation* is necessary. Even the great Howlin' Wolf took classes to learn this way of writing and reading music.

PITCH

Pitch is the aspect of standard music notation that indicates the degree of highness or lowness of a musical tone.

Notes

Music is written by placing *notes* on a *staff*. Notes appear in various ways.

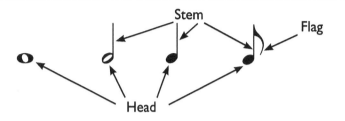

The Staff and Clef

The staff has five lines and four spaces which are read from left to right. At the beginning of the staff is a *clef*. The clef dictates what notes correspond to a particular line or space on the staff. Guitar music is written in *treble clef* 𝄞 which is sometimes called the *G clef*. The ending curl of the clef circles the G line on the staff.

Here are the notes on the staff using the G clef.

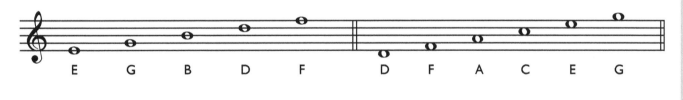

Ledger Lines

The higher a note appears on the staff, the higher it sounds. When a note is too high or too low to be written on the staff, *ledger lines* are used.

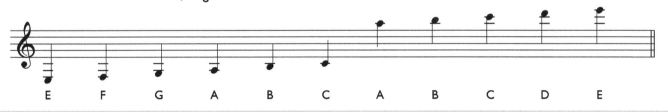

For reasons of convenience and easy reading, guitar music is written one octave higher than it sounds.

TIME

Musical time is measured in *beats*. Beats are the steady pulse of the music on which we build *rhythms*. Rhythm is a pattern of long and short sounds and silences and is represented by *note* and *rest values*. Value indicates duration.

Measures and Bar Lines

The staff is divided by vertical lines called *bar lines*. The space between two bar lines is a *measure* or *bar*. Measures divide music into groups of beats. A *double bar* marks the end of a section or example.

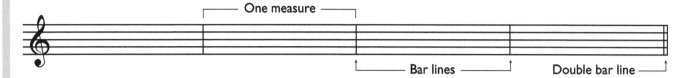

Note Values

The duration of a note—its value—is indicated by the note's appearance or shape.

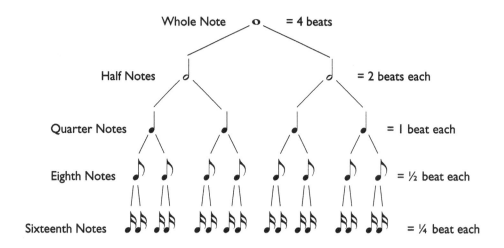

Time Signatures

A *time signature* appears at the beginning of a piece of music. The number on top indicates the number of beats per measure. The number on the bottom indicates the type of note that gets one beat.

$\frac{4}{4}$ = 4 beats per measure
Quarter note ♩ = one beat

$\frac{3}{4}$ = 3 beats per measure
Quarter note ♩ = one beat

$\frac{6}{8}$ = 6 beats per measure
Eighth note ♪ = one beat

Sometimes a **C** is used in place of $\frac{4}{4}$.
This is called *common time*.

Rest Values

Every note value has a corresponding *rest* value. A rest indicates silence in music. A *whole rest* indicates four beats of silence, a *half rest* is two beats of silence, etc.

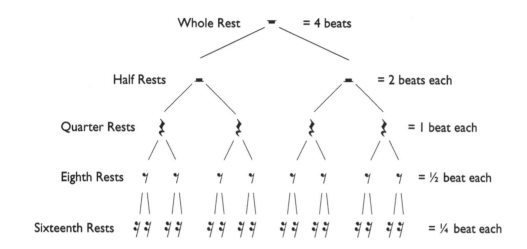

Beaming

Notes that are less than one beat in duration are often *beamed* together. Sometimes they are grouped in twos and sometimes they are grouped in fours.

Ties and Counting

A *tie* is a curved line that joins two or more notes of the same pitch that last the duration of the combined note values. For example, when a half note (two beats) is tied to a quarter note (one beat), the combined notes are held for three beats (2 + 1 = 3).

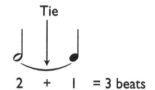

Notice the numbers under the staff in the examples below. These indicate how to count while playing. Both of these examples are in $\frac{4}{4}$ time, so we count four beats in each measure. *Eighth-note* rhythms are counted "1–&, 2–&, 3–&," etc. The numbers are the *onbeats* and the "&"s (pronounced "and") are the *offbeats*.

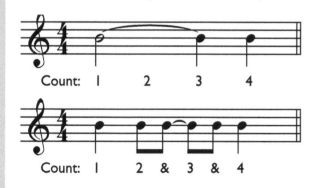

Dots

A *dot* increases the length of a note or rest by one half of its original value. For instance, a half note lasts for two beats. Half of its value is one beat (a quarter note). So a *dotted half note* equals three beats (2 + 1 = 3), which is the same as a half note tied to a quarter note. The same logic applies for all dotted notes.

Dotted notes are especially important when the time signature is $\frac{3}{4}$, because the longest note value that will fit in a measure is a dotted half note. Also, dotted notes are very important in $\frac{6}{8}$ time, because not only is a dotted half note the longest possible note value, but a dotted quarter note is exactly half of a measure (counted: 1–&–ah, 2–&–ah).

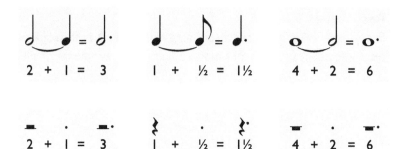

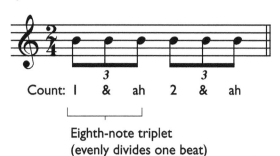

Triplets

A *triplet* is three notes in the time of two, or a group of three notes that, together, make up one unit of musical time, such as a beat.

Eighth-note triplet
(evenly divides one beat)

Repeat Signs

Repeat signs are used to indicate music that should be repeated.

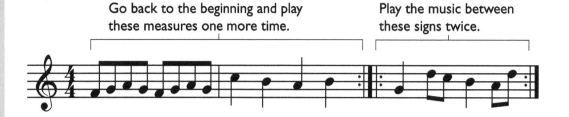

This sign ‰ tells us to repeat the previous measure.

Tablature, or TAB, is an alternative form of music notation used for guitar and other fretted string instruments. In various forms, it has been in existence for hundreds of years. Tablature tells you the location, on the fretboard, of each note to be played. It provides string and fret numbers, whereas standard music notation provides pitches only—it is the guitarist's choice where to play any given pitch (on the guitar there are many places where any particular pitch can be played). Tablature, when combined with standard music notation, provides the most complete system for communicating the many possibilities in guitar playing.

Rhythm is not indicated in TAB; for that, you must refer to the standard music notation.

Six lines are used to indicate the six strings of the guitar. The top line is the high-E string and the bottom line is the low-E string.

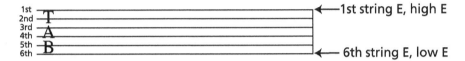

Numbers are placed on these lines to indicate frets. If there is a "0," play that string open. The fingers of the left hand are numbered 1–4, starting with the index finger. Left-hand fingerings are indicated underneath the TAB staff.

In the following example, the first note is played with the 1st finger on the 1st fret of the 1st string. The next note is played with the 2nd finger on the 2nd fret of the 1st string. The next note is the open 1st string and the last note is played with the 4th finger on the 4th fret of the 1st string.

Left-hand finger numbers.

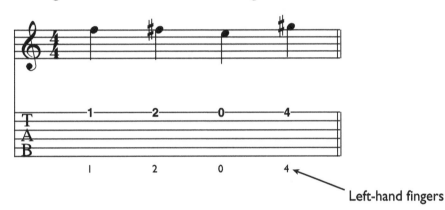

Left-hand fingers

In TAB, a tied note is written in parentheses.

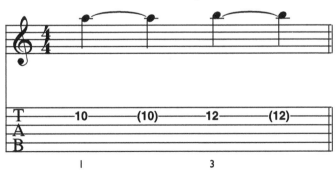

SCALE DIAGRAMS

A *scale* is an arrangement of pitches in a particular order of whole steps and half steps. A *scale diagram* illustrates the pitches of a scale that are to be played one at a time, in succession.

Scale diagrams are oriented horizontally. The horizontal lines represent the strings. The vertical lines represent the frets. Dots tell us where to place our fingers on the fretboard.

Scale diagrams are read bottom-to-top, left-to-right. For example, in the diagram below, we would start with 6th string, 5th fret. Then we would go to the 6th string, 8th fret. Then to the 5th string, 5th fret—5th string, 7th fret—4th string, 5th fret—and then end on the 4th string, 7th fret.

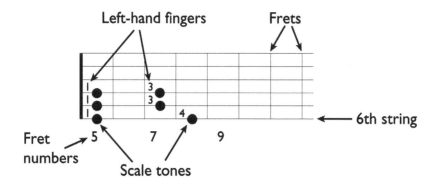

CHORD DIAGRAMS

A *chord* is three or more tones played simultaneously. A *chord diagram* shows how it is to be played. Chord diagrams are oriented vertically. The vertical lines represent the strings. The horizontal lines represent frets.

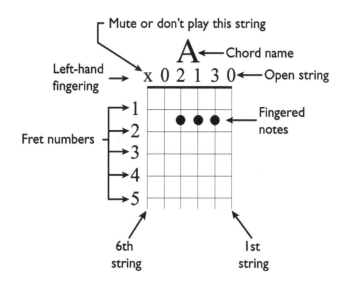

A *chord chart* is a way of writing the *chord progression* (series of chords) for a song or piece of music. It does not give the *melody* or tune of the composition, just the chord changes. The chords are written above the staff. Sometimes, the strum or rhythm is written on the staff below the chord names in *slash notation* (which does not specify rhythm).

Chord Chart (Slash Notation)

Sometimes, *rhythmic notation* is used. This is a way of conveying rhythm without pitch.

Chord Chart (Rhythmic Notation)

Here are the rhythmic notation values.

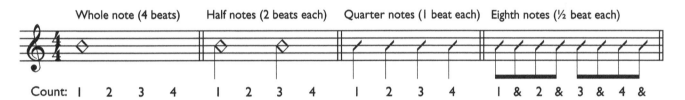

This symbol ⊓ signifies a *downstroke*; it tells us to strum or pick downward (toward the floor). This symbol ∨ signifies an *upstroke*; it tells us to strum or pick upward (toward the ceiling). When strumming down, strike all of the chord tones. When strumming up, strike only the first few strings (those closest to the floor). The upstrums should sound lighter than the downstrums.

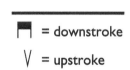

⊓ = downstroke

∨ = upstroke

When it is assumed you know how a chord is to be played, only the chord name is given.

Posture is very important when playing guitar. Sit or stand up straight. This will help you avoid back problems and fatigue. Do not strain; your hands, arms and shoulders should be loose and relaxed.

Here are the proper playing positions.

Standing with guitar strap.

Sitting with strap.

When sitting, use a strap to elevate the neck to a 45 degree angle, to simulate how it would be if you were standing. This will keep your wrists straight and give you easy access to the neck.

RIGHT-HAND TECHNIQUE

There is no *one* correct right-hand approach when playing acoustic blues. One approach is to *strum* the strings. This is accomplished by moving rapidly across the strings with either the thumb or a guitar pick (also called *flatpick*). Picks come in various shapes and thicknesses. It is advisable to use a medium or heavy gauge pick in the standard triangular shape with rounded edges. The thicker the pick, the fuller the sound that is produced. You want a full, fat sound for the blues. Thinner picks work well for pop or folk/rock style strumming, but sound thin when playing single notes or blues rhythms. Some players use combinations of their thumb and fingers or even a guitar pick and fingers. Other players use a *country blues style,* which is a total *fingerpicking* approach (see page 85, Fingerstyle Blues).

The right hand should be placed near or over the soundhole.

Most of the exercises in this book are intended to be played with a pick. This is the most common approach and will give you an appropriate sound in most situations. However, you are also encouraged to play the exercises with your bare thumb. A pick will give you a clear sound with a hard edge. The thumb will give you a sound that is softer and rounder or "fatter." You will be a more versatile guitarist if you are accustomed to both ways of playing. It is one factor in achieving the best sound you can for each song you play.

LEFT-HAND TECHNIQUE

When fretting the strings, place your left-hand fingers just to the left of the fret wire—never on top of it. Curve them slightly and do not press too hard. If a tone is not clear, the problem is most likely bad finger placement, not insufficient force. If your guitar seems unusually difficult to play, have a repair person take a look at it.

A good left-hand position.

Position your thumb in the center of the back of the neck.

Thumb behind the neck.

CHAPTER 2

12-Bar Blues Progressions

The standard musical form used in the blues is the *12-bar blues progression*. It is 12 bars (measures) long and is almost always in $\frac{4}{4}$ time. Although there are many variations, it consists of three chords that progress in standard patterns. In this chapter, you'll learn two of the most important versions of the 12-bar blues.

EASIEST 12-BAR BLUES

The following chord progression is the most basic 12-bar blues form and the easiest to play. Throughout this book we will refer to it as the "Easiest Blues" form.

Here are the three chords you will need to play this progression.

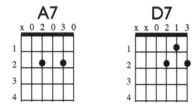
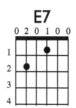

If you are unfamiliar with any of these chords, practice changing from one to another, back and forth, repeatedly. It takes time and consistent practice for new chords to become comfortable.

All the examples in this chapter are to be played with a simple quarter-note strum rhythm: one strum for each beat. With each strum, count the beat numbers aloud and tap your foot. Make sure that the beats are all equal in duration and the *tempo*, or speed, is steady and consistent.

 EASIEST 12-BAR BLUES

Track 2

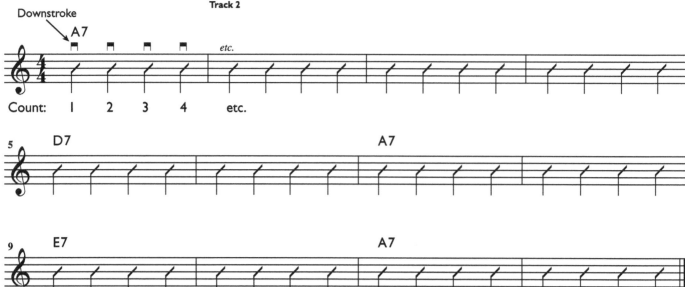

To understand what is happening musically in the blues progression you just played, let's look at some music theory.

SCALES

A *scale* is a series of notes arranged in a specific order of whole steps and half steps. The notes of a scale ascend and descend in alphabetical order (remember, the musical alphabet is the first seven letters of the English alphabet, A through G). Each note in the scale is a *scale degree*. The scale degrees are numbered upward from the lowest note.

MAJOR SCALES

A *major scale* is made up of eight notes with half steps between the 3rd and 4th, and 7th and 8th degrees. The distance between the rest are whole steps. The scale takes its name from its lowest note (1st degree or *tonic*). The eight notes of the scale span an octave. The 8th degree is an octave above the 1st degree. Study the placement of whole and half steps represented by the letters "W" and "H" in the example on the right.

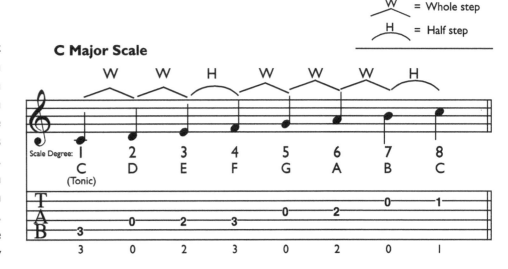

CHORDS COME FROM SCALES

The chords we use to play the blues are derived from the major scale. Remember that a chord is three or more notes played together. We create a *triad*, the most basic kind of chord, by simply using every other note in a major scale. For example, to the right is how we build a C Major chord:

In the blues, we usually need only three chords for any tune: a chord built on the 1st degree (the *I* chord—Roman numerals are used to refer to chords), the 4th degree (the *IV* chord) and the 5th degree (the *V* chord). In the illustration to the right, these chords are shown in the *key* (the set of notes and chords of a scale) of C:

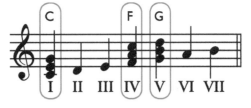

I or i	1
II or ii	2
III or iii	3
IV or iv	4
V or v	5
VI or vi	6
VII or vii	7

EASIEST BLUES FORM—ANALYSIS

The Easiest 12-Bar Blues (page 20) is in the key of A, which means the notes of the melody and the chords are all from the A Major scale. The chords built from the 1st, 4th and 5th scale degrees are A7(I), D7(IV) and E7(V). Note that in the blues, chords are often made into "7" chords (covered in detail on pages 39–40) for more of a bluesy feel.

The Easiest Blues form should be memorized, as it is the standard form for the 12-bar blues. It consists of:

- Four bars of I
- Two bars of IV
- Two bars of I
- Two bars of V
- Two bars of I

Now let's play this same progression in the key of E. This is the most common of all blues keys. The pattern for the Roman numerals are the same, but the chords themselves are different. The I, IV and V—or *primary chords*—in the key of E are E7(I), A7(IV) and B7(V).

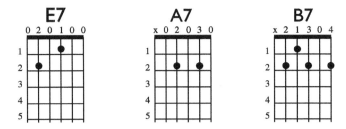

Work on the B7 chord for awhile. It can be challenging at first because you are fretting a note with your 4th finger, but you need to master this very common blues chord.

 ## EASIEST 12-BAR BLUES IN E
Track 3

I ← Roman numerals for chords above staff

IV   I

V   I

BACKBEAT

In the blues (as well as rock and other popular styles), all beats are not created equal. Most blues tunes are in $\frac{4}{4}$, with four beats per bar. To create a rhythmic pulse, accent (or strum louder on) the 2nd and 4th beats in each bar. This emphasis on the 2nd and 4th beats is called a *backbeat*. It should be your standard approach throughout this book.

MOST COMMON 12-BAR BLUES

Chord movements in songs are called *changes*. The most common 12-bar blues progression —referred to throughout this book as the "Most Common Blues"—has a few more changes than the Easiest Blues form. There is a quick change from the I chord in the 1st bar to the IV chord in the 2nd bar and back again to the I in the 3rd bar. This is called a *quick IV*. There are other changes in the last four bars as well.

The repeat sign in the 12th measure tells us to repeat the progression from the beginning and then play the last two bars. Of course, at a gig or at a jam session, you'll be playing through any progression more than twice. The 12-bar progression is repeated numerous times as a singer sings and musicians solo. Each run through the 12-bar form is a *chorus*. At the very end, we usually add a bar or two of the I chord to give a sense of finality to the piece.

Track 4

MOST COMMON 12-BAR BLUES IN A

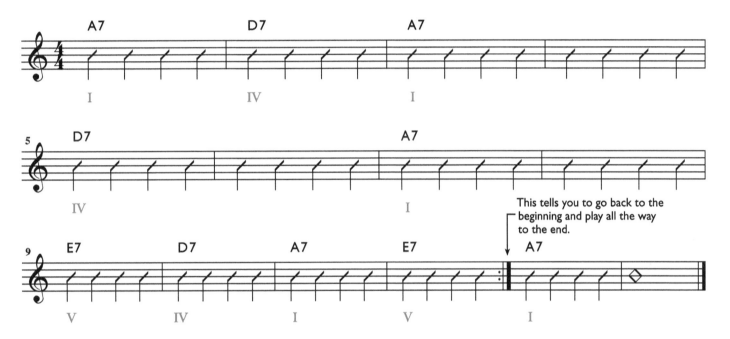

This tells you to go back to the beginning and play all the way to the end.

To summarize, the Most Common Blues progression consists of:

- One bar of I
- One bar of IV
- Two bars of I
- Two bars of IV
- Two bars of I
- One bar of V
- One bar of IV
- One bar of I
- One bar of V
- At the very end, two bars of I

This should also be memorized as it is the most widely used form of the 12-bar blues.

Now let's play the Most Common Blues form in the key of E. It is important to memorize the Easiest and Most Common Blues forms in the keys of A and E and, eventually, all the common keys.

 MOST COMMON 12-BAR BLUES IN E
Track 5

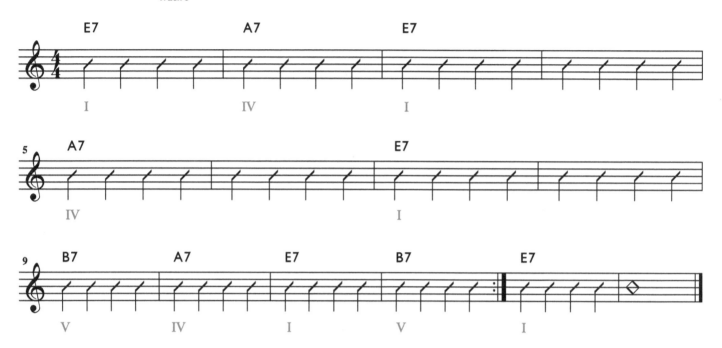

Notice that, though the chords are different from the progression in the key of A, the Roman numeral pattern is the same.

Son House (1902-1988). His song "Death Letter" is a classic example of the Delta Blues style, which is often characterized by a solo singer accompanying himself on a guitar. The blues historian Alan Lomax recorded Son House in 1941 in Lake Coromont, Mississippi for the Library of Congress archives.

PHOTO COURTESY OF STAR FILE PHOTO, INC.

While the keys of A and E are the most popular for guitar-based blues, there are other keys that are widely used as well.

The primary chords in the key of D are D7(I), G7(IV) and A7(V).

MOST COMMON 12-BAR BLUES IN D

Track 6

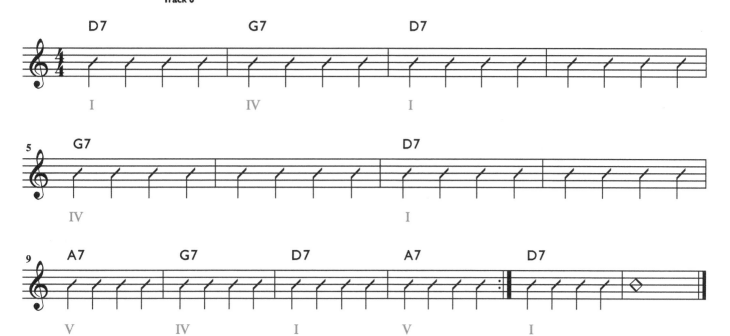

The primary chords in the key of G are G7(I), C7(IV) and D7(V).

  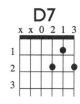

MOST COMMON 12-BAR BLUES IN G

Track 7

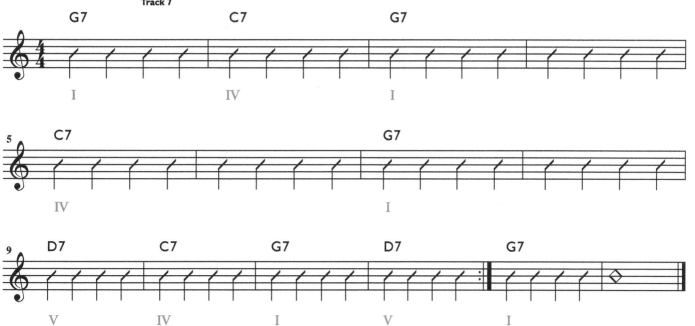

CHAPTER 3

Blues Rhythm & Theory

SWING EIGHTHS

In blues (and jazz also), eighth notes are not usually played exactly as notated. Rather, they are interpreted in what is called a *swing* or *shuffle* style. This makes a pair of eighth notes sound like the first and last notes of a triplet (page 14). This is important to know, since almost every example in this book is in swing style. *Swing eighths* look exactly like "straight eighths," but we play them in swing style. In this book, this swing rhythm is indicated with the caption: *Swing 8ths.*

Written and counted: Played:

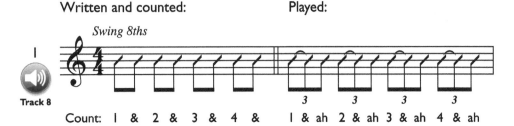

Track 8

If you were to run down the street, the rhythm your feet make would be straight eighths. If you were to skip down the street, you would be skipping with a swing or shuffle rhythm, where the first step of each pair is longer than the second: long-short, long-short, long-short. So try running and skipping down the street and just tell your friends you are practicing blues rhythm!

INTERVALS

The major scale is the standard by which many musical concepts can be understood. To use the scale this way, it is important to understand *intervals*. An interval is the distance between two pitches. You already know two intervals: the whole step and the half step.

Every pitch in a major scale can be understood in terms of its interval from the tonic. The second degree, for example, is an interval of a 2nd (2) above the tonic. The third degree is an interval of a 3rd (3) above the tonic, and so on. The same note sounded more than once is a *unison*.

Every interval has a *quality*. It is either *major*, *minor*, *perfect*, *diminished* or *augmented*. All of the pitches in a major scale, when measured from the tonic, create perfect or major intervals.

P = Perfect
M = Major

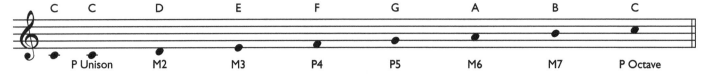

A major interval can be changed to a minor interval using an accidental. For example, C–E is a major 3rd, so C–E♭ is a minor 3rd. Other intervals can be changed this way, too.

CHAPTER 4

Blues Shuffles

Until now, we have played the Easiest and Most Common Blues progressions with quarter-note strums: one strum for every beat. This works fine in many cases. Knowing when to keep it simple is important in the blues. But you need to learn other important rhythms as well. *Shuffle style,* which is played with swing eighths (page 26) is one of the most widely used rhythms in blues, rock and even country music.

TWO-STRING CHORDS

"5" CHORDS

A *5 chord* is made up of two notes on the lower strings. They are really just *intervals* of a perfect 5th (see page 26). To the right is a diagram of an A5 chord. Its two notes are A on the open 5th string, and E on the 2nd fret of the 4th string. In an A Major scale, A is the 1st scale degree and E is the 5th. Because of this, it is called A5.

A5

It's common for players to base their entire approach around these chords, as with punk, hard rock or metal styles. They create a strong sound and in this context they are called *power chords.*

With all two-string chords, be sure to strum only the two strings that are indicated. This can be a little tricky at first, but if you are hitting unwanted strings, you will not get the right sound. You can mute the 3rd string by leaning your 1st finger against it.

Play the exercise below—and all the pieces in this chapter—using downstrokes only; it's the standard approach for this two-string style. Also, be sure to tap your foot on the onbeats (the numbers) and count: 1–&, 2–&, 3–&, 4–&, etc.

Remember, this is played with swing eighths, so the eighth notes are more like the first and last notes of an eighth-note triplet.

A *key signature* is at the beginning of every line of music and tells you which notes are sharp or flat throughout the piece. You can tell what key you are in by the number of sharps or flats. The key of A has three sharps.

Key signature

Track 9

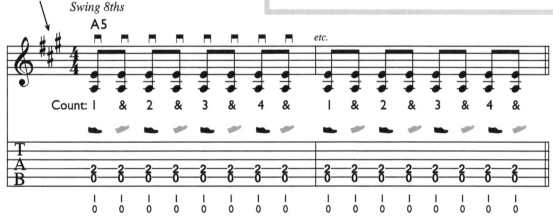

"6" CHORDS

We can now tweak these "5" chords by moving the fretted note one whole step up on the fretboard. This new note is the interval of a major 6th from the bottom note so it is called a "6" chord. For example, to the right is a diagram of an A6 chord. It consists of A on the open 5th string and F# on the 4th fret of the 4th string. In an A Major scale, A is the 1st scale degree and F# is the 6th. Because of this, it is called A6.

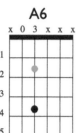

Notice that the A6 chord diagram to the right shows two notes fretted on the 4th string. The gray dot is telling you to keep your 1st finger on the 2nd fret while also fretting the 4th fret with your 3rd finger. Although the E on the 2nd fret will not be heard when fretting the F# on the 4th fret, you'll be alternating between the "5" and "6" forms.

Below is an exercise to get you started with this.

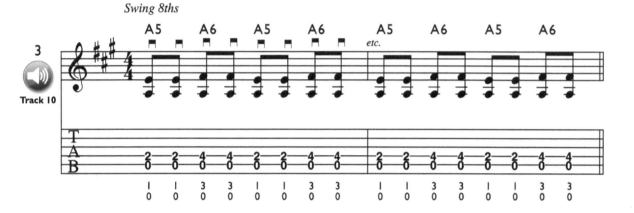

Taj Mahal (born Henry St. Clair Fredericks) was a major force in the blues revival of the 1960s. A champion of traditional acoustic blues, he has also infused his unique style with roots and folk music from all over the world.

Let's apply this technique to the 4th and 3rd strings. This gives us D5 and D6.

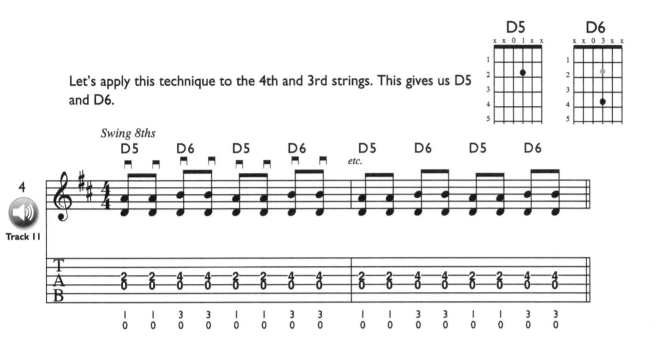

Now let's apply this to the 6th and 5th strings. This gives us E5 and E6.

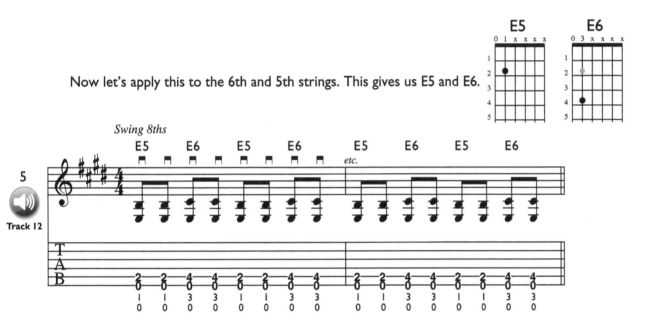

Every leading blues artist has played in this style. Some, like Jimmy Reed, have used it in almost all of their songs.

Normally, in songs featuring this two-string shuffle style, only the general chord sound is written above the staff. So, instead of an alternating A5–A6–A5–A6, you will see only A.

Now let's apply this technique to an entire blues form. Below is the Easiest Blues played in this cool double-note shuffle style.

SHUFFLE BLUES IN A

Chords in gray show the general sound of the music and are not necessarily meant to be played.

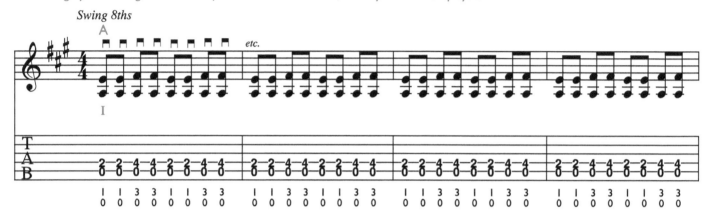

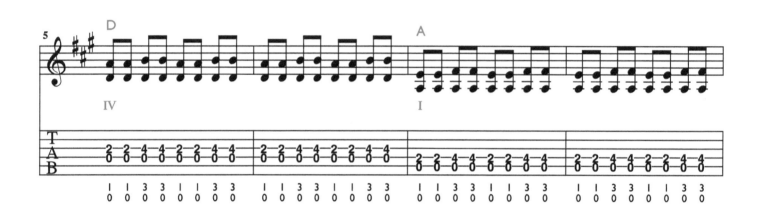

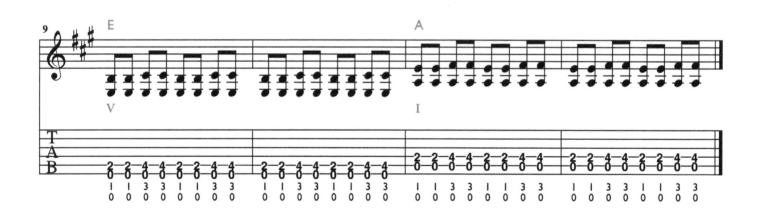

THE FLAT-7

We use the term "flat" loosely in this context to mean "lower a half step." For example, if we flat a G♯, we get a G♮. G♯ is the 7th scale degree in the A Major scale, so G♮ is considered a ♭7 (flat-7).

Below is a variation on the alternating "5" and "6" chord pattern. If you use the 4th finger of your left hand to go one fret higher than the 6th, you will be playing a ♭7. This is an essential blues sound.

This shuffle uses the Most Common Blues form.

THE 5, 6, ♭7 BLUES IN A

Track 14

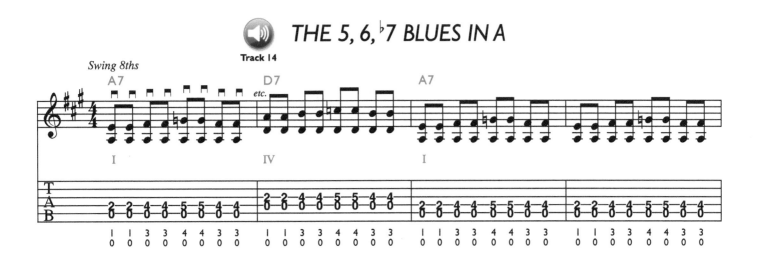

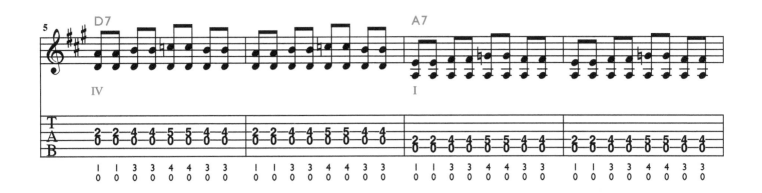

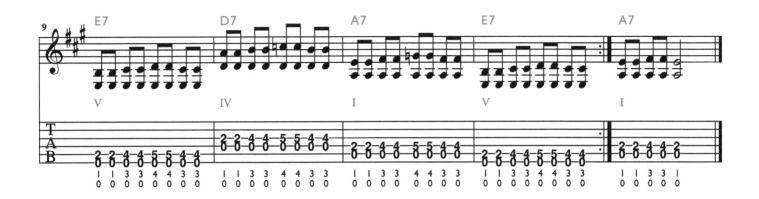

Chapter 4—Blues Shuffles   **31**

The following piece is a Most Common Blues in the key of E. It combines two-string variations of "5," "6" and "♭7" chords with full chords. Strum the full chords in bars 9, 10 and 12 with a down-up pattern. Strum all the strings in the chord on the downstrokes, but give less emphasis to the upstrokes, strumming only the first few strings. Notice in the last measure that, in TAB, tied notes are in parentheses.

Track 15

SHUFFLE BLUES IN E

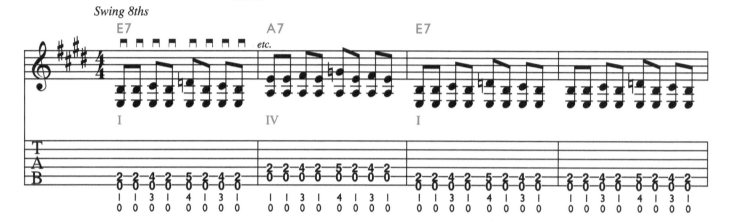

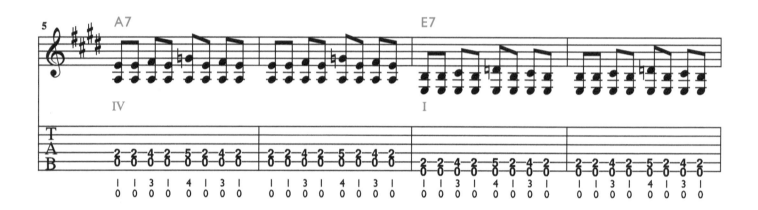

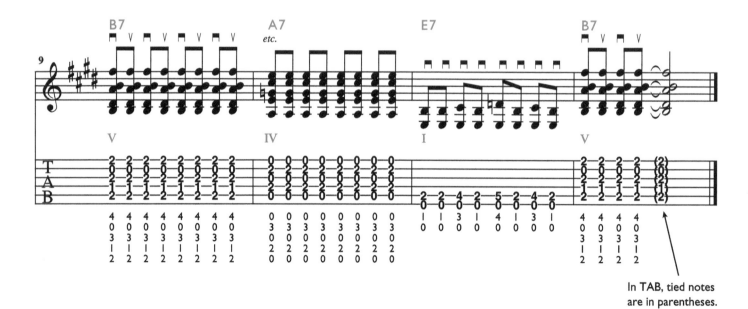

In TAB, tied notes are in parentheses.

CHAPTER 5

Palm Muting

Now that you've played your first blues shuffle, let's look at a right-hand technique that is used very often in this style. It's called *palm muting* and is quite easy once you get the hang of it.

For this technique, your hand must be positioned at the *bridge* (the piece that is glued to the front part of the guitar body, where the strings are anchored—see photo to the right).

Notice that the strings go right over the *saddle* (the thin white plastic piece that sits on the bridge). Place the lower left part, or *heel,* of your right hand on the saddle where the lower strings rest. Do not press too hard. Just rest your hand. We merely want to dampen the sound of the strings, not cut them out entirely.

Right-hand position for palm muting.

Experiment with the pressure and placement. Don't go too far back or too far forward. You should be resting right where the strings hit the saddle.

Use this new technique on the example below. Try to match the sound on the recording. It's a sound you've heard on many a blues, rock and country tune.

SHUFFLIN' THE PALM MUTE

Track 16

P.M.= Palm mute

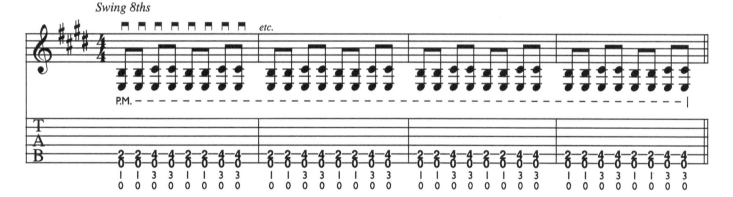

The next piece uses the Most Common Blues form. It uses a variation on the alternating "5" and "6" chord pattern. In each group of four strums, you strum the "5" chord twice, then the "6" chord once, then the "5" chord once more. So the pattern is 5–5–6–5, 5–5–6–5, etc.

Because we are using straight eighths rather than swing eighths, it is not considered a shuffle. Many blues tunes use this steady rhythm rather than the shuffle rhythm. You need to be able to play in swing and steady eighth-note style, and to feel the difference between the two rhythms. This can be challenging for many beginning players. A way to develop this ability is to listen to—and play along with—the recording that accompanies this book. Also, when listening to other music, try to distinguish whether the rhythm is in swing or straight-eighth style.

PALM MUTING IN A

Track 17

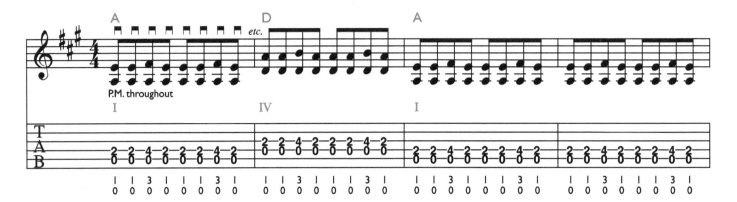

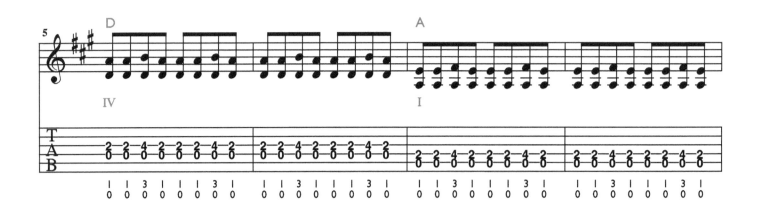

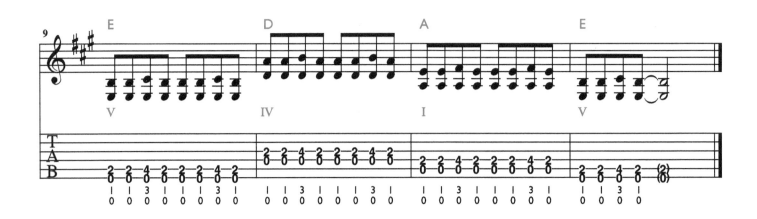

CHAPTER 6

Major Scale Theory Review

We have already taken our first look at the major scale (page 21). Because it is the standard by which we can understand many other musical concepts, we must now take a closer look.

Oddly enough, it is more important for a blues player to know major scale theory than to be able to play major scales on the guitar. The reason for this is that they are generally not used in the blues style.

Remember, a scale is a series of notes arranged in a particular pattern of whole steps and half steps. The major scale is made up of a series of seven notes. The note that follows the 7th note, or scale degree, is the octave of the tonic. You may be familiar with this scale in the form of the famous "doh–re–mi–fa–so–la–ti–doh" sequence.

As you learned on page 21, the major scale is made up of whole steps and half steps in this order: **Whole–Whole–Half–Whole–Whole–Whole–Half, or W–W–H–W–W–W–H.** The sentence "**W**endy **W**itch **H**as **W**ild **W**onderful **W**avy **H**air" can help you remember this pattern of whole and half steps.

If we start this pattern for a major scale with C as our tonic, our notes are C–D–E–F–G–A–B–C.

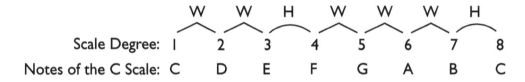 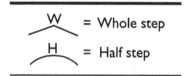

Let's play the C Major scale. Here it is in standard music notation and TAB.

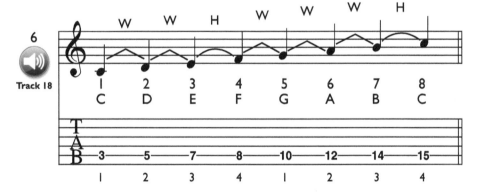

Here is a fretboard diagram of the C Major scale on one string.

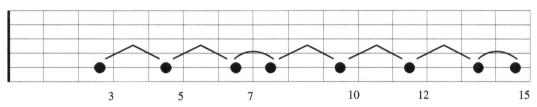

A major scale, like any scale, can start on any note. The chart below contains the notes for almost every major scale.

The Major Scale							
1	2	3	4	5	6	7	8
C	D	E	F	G	A	B	C
G	A	B	C	D	E	F#	G
D	E	F#	G	A	B	C#	D
A	B	C#	D	E	F#	G#	A
E	F#	G#	A	B	C#	D#	E
B	C#	D#	E	F#	G#	A#	B
F#	G#	A#	B	C#	D#	E#	F#
G♭	A♭	B♭	C♭	D♭	E♭	F	G♭
D♭	E♭	F	G♭	A♭	B♭	C	D♭
A♭	B♭	C	D♭	E♭	F	G	A♭
E♭	F	G	A♭	B♭	C	D	E♭
B♭	C	D	E♭	F	G	A	B♭
F	G	A	B♭	C	D	E	F

Scale degrees →

These scales are enharmonic equivalents. (→ pointing to F# row and G♭ row)

Though the F# Major and G♭ Major scales have different names, they sound exactly the same. These two scales consist of notes that share the same pitches, but have different names. Remember, when two notes have the same pitch, but different names, they are enharmonic equivalents (see page 9, Accidentals) .

CHAPTER 7

Chord Theory and Key Signatures

With our understanding of the major scale, we can now take a closer look at how chords are built and how they fit into different keys. It may be helpful to review page 26 (Intervals) before reading this chapter.

MAJOR AND MINOR TRIADS

Remember, a chord is the combination of three (or more) different notes. The most basic chords are three-note chords called triads. *Major* and *minor triads* are the most commonly used chords. Keep in mind that the word "major" is only *implied* when talking about major chords. For example, if you are talking about a G Major chord, you would call it a "G" chord. Triads are built by stacking pitches in 3rds.

Let's build a C Major triad. C is the *root* (1) of the chord; E is a 3rd above C, so it is called the 3rd (3) of the chord; G is a 3rd above E and 5th above C, so it is called the 5th (5) of the chord. Like all major triads, it consists of a major 3rd on the bottom and a minor 3rd on the top.

M = Major
m = Minor

You can use the 1, 3 and 5 of any major scale to build a major triad. Lower the 3rd (♭3) of any major triad, or you can think in terms of lowering the 3rd of the scale, and you have a minor triad. Notice that it is a minor 3rd from the 1 to the ♭3 and a major 3rd from the ♭3 to the 5.

DIMINISHED AND AUGMENTED TRIADS

Though they are not used as often as the major and minor, there are two other kinds of triads: *diminished* and *augmented*. A diminished triad consists of two minor 3rds and an augmented triad consists of two major 3rds. In a diminished triad, the 5th is a diminished 5th (or $\flat$5), or "d5." In an augmented triad the 5th is an augmented 5th (or $\sharp$5), or "A5."

A = Augmented
d = Diminished

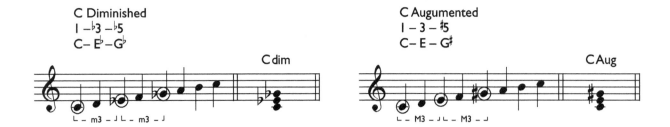

So, to get a diminished chord (abbreviated as *dim,* or designated with this symbol ○) lower the 5th of a minor triad a half step. To get an augmented chord (abbreviated as *Aug,* or designated with this symbol +), raise the 5th of a major triad a half step.

Chord Voicings

A *voicing* is the way the notes of a chord are stacked or arranged. So far in this chapter, we've looked at simple three-note chords. In common practice, some of these notes are doubled or even tripled in different octaves. This gives us a fuller sound than a three-note voicing.

Jimmy Reed had a sweet and easily accessible sound that has been widely appreciated and imitated. Playing harp in a mouth rack as he played guitar, he had hit after hit on the R&B and pop charts in the 1960s. This was a rare feat by a pure bluesman which has perhaps only been surpassed by B. B. King. His sweet, yearning vocals and relaxed, laid-back blues have inspired many rock bands and solo acoustic artists.

PHOTO COURTESY OF HOHNER, INC.

7 CHORDS

A "7" chord is built by stacking another 3rd on top of an existing triad. The interval from the root to this added note is a 7th. So the intervals of a 7 chord are 1–3–5–7.

There are many types of 7 chords. We'll look at those most commonly used in the blues.

MAJOR 7 CHORDS

A *major 7 chord* (Maj7) is made by placing a major 3rd above a major triad. This additional note is the interval of a major 7th (M7) from the root. The intervals of this chord are 1–3–5–7.

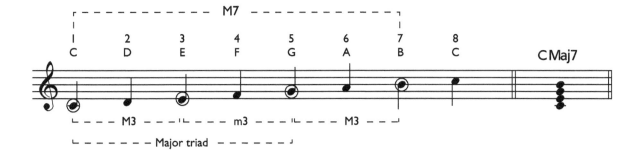

MINOR 7 CHORDS

A *minor 7 chord* (min7) is made by placing a minor 3rd above a minor triad. This additional note is the interval of a minor 7th (m7) from the root. The intervals of this chord are 1–♭3–5–♭7.

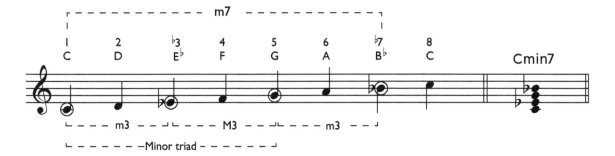

DOMINANT 7 CHORDS

The most commonly used 7 chord in the blues is the *dominant 7*. A dominant 7 chord is designated by a "7" (for example, A7, D7 and G7). It is made by placing a minor 3rd above a major triad. This additional note is the interval of a minor 7th from the root. The intervals of this chord are 1–3–5–♭7.

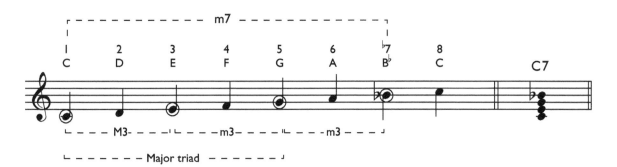

The next two types of 7 chords (like the triads they are built on) are not as common as the preceding ones. They can, however, be very effective when used at the right time.

HALF DIMINISHED 7 CHORDS

A *half diminished 7 chord* (min7♭5) is made by placing a major 3rd above a diminished triad. This additional note is the interval of a minor 7th from the root. The intervals of this chord are 1–♭3–♭5–♭7.

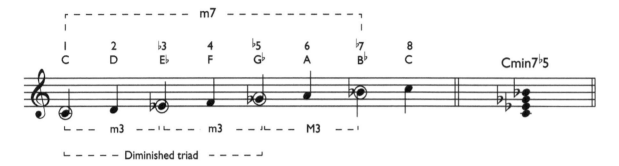

DIMINISHED 7 CHORDS

A *diminished 7 chord* (dim7) is made by placing a minor 3rd above a diminished triad. This additional note is the interval of a diminished 7th (which is a half step lower than a minor 7th) from the root. The intervals of this chord are 1–♭3–♭5–♭♭7.*

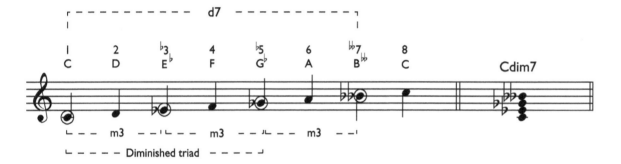

---

* A *double flat* ♭♭ is used to lower a note two half steps, or a whole step. This particular note (B♭♭) is the enharmonic equivalent of A.

DIATONIC HARMONY

Now we will see how chords relate to keys. Each major scale has its unique set of notes. Each note is the root of a corresponding chord. A key is the set of all the notes and chords of a scale. These notes and chords are *diatonic*, which means they belong to the key. *Diatonic harmony* refers to the chords that belong to a particular key.

To build the chords in a major key we start with the major scale. Taking each note in the scale as a root (remember to count the root as 1), we skip a note to find the 3rd and—from the 3rd—skip another note to find the 5th. Here are the chords in the key of C:

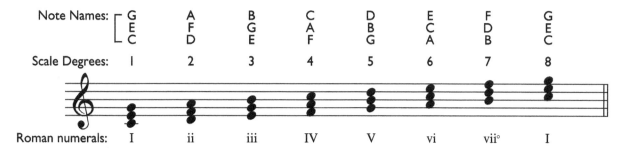

Note Names:	G E C	A F D	B G E	C A F	D B G	E C A	F D B	G E C
Scale Degrees:	1	2	3	4	5	6	7	8
Roman numerals:	I	ii	iii	IV	V	vi	vii°	I

As discussed on page 21, Roman numerals are used to represent each chord. Uppercase is used for major chords (I, IV, V—the primary chords) and lowercase is used for minor and diminished chords (ii, iii, vi, vii). This sign ○ is used to show that a chord is diminished (vii°).

The diatonic pattern of major, minor and diminished chords is the same in every major key.

I	ii	iii	IV	V	vi	vii°	I
major	minor	minor	major	major	minor	diminished	major

- The I, IV and V chords are always major.
- The ii, iii and vi chords are always minor.
- The vii° is always diminished.

For the sake of convenience, musicians refer to the chords of a key by their Roman numerals. You might hear a guitarist say: "It's a ii–V–I progression in the key of E." Knowing this system can help you when playing with other musicians. The primary chords are by far the most common chords in the blues. The chart to the right will help you learn these in each key. Memorize the natural note keys first, as these are the easiest.

As mentioned on page 21 (Easiest Blues Form—Analysis), in the blues we usually add the ♭7 to our I, IV and V chords to get a dominant 7 sound. The ♭7s of the I and IV chords are not diatonic notes to the major scale based on the I chord, but adding them helps to create a "bluesy" sound that is fundamental to this style.

I	IV	V
C	F	G
G	C	D
D	G	A
A	D	E
E	A	B
B	E	F♯
F♯	B	C♯
G♭	C♭	D♭
D♭	G♭	A♭
A♭	D♭	E♭
E♭	A♭	B♭
B♭	E♭	F
F	B♭	C

KEY SIGNATURES

A key signature is placed after the clef on each line of music. It indicates which notes are sharp or flat—in all octaves—throughout a piece of music. The accidentals that appear in the key signature are those in the major scale of the same name. The number of sharps or flats indicates the key the music is in. The key of C Major has no sharps or flats.

Key signature

Sharp Keys

Flat Keys

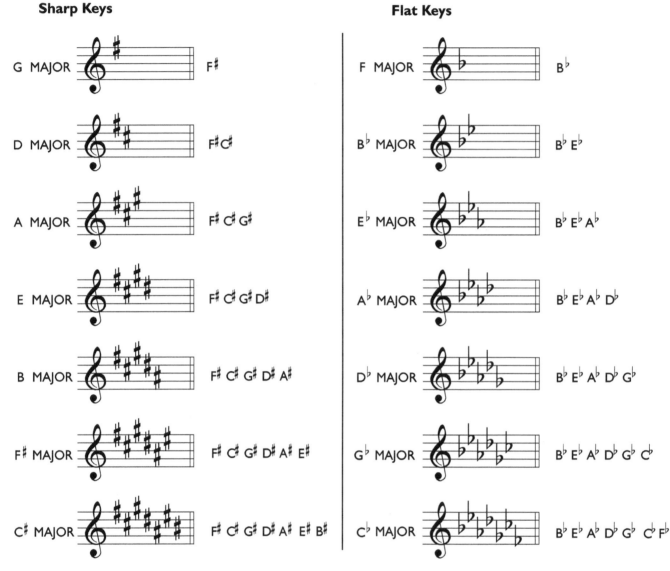

G MAJOR — F#

D MAJOR — F# C#

A MAJOR — F# C# G#

E MAJOR — F# C# G# D#

B MAJOR — F# C# G# D# A#

F# MAJOR — F# C# G# D# A# E#

C# MAJOR — F# C# G# D# A# E# B#

F MAJOR — B♭

B♭ MAJOR — B♭ E♭

E♭ MAJOR — B♭ E♭ A♭

A♭ MAJOR — B♭ E♭ A♭ D♭

D♭ MAJOR — B♭ E♭ A♭ D♭ G♭

G♭ MAJOR — B♭ E♭ A♭ D♭ G♭ C♭

C♭ MAJOR — B♭ E♭ A♭ D♭ G♭ C♭ F♭

Knowing key signatures can help us learn songs by ear, because we come to know what notes or chords to expect in a key. Most often, the letter name of the first chord in a song will also be the name of the key.

CHAPTER 8

Boogie Woogie Blues Patterns

Boogie woogie is a blues piano style in which a pianist plays a steady eighth-note pattern with the left hand, and chords and melody with the right hand. The eighth-note pattern, which is based on the major scale, usually proceeds from the tonic, to the 3rd, to the 5th, then to the 6th and/or ♭7th. This pattern is played ascending and then descending (for example, 1–3–5–6–♭7–6–5–3, etc.). Guitarists, who have been copying this style for a long time, usually just play the left-hand part on the lower strings.

CLOSED FORMS

Our first boogie woogie piece uses the Easiest Blues form and is in the key of G. Notice, in the TAB, it is made up entirely of fretted notes—no open strings. This sort of *closed* form allows for easy *transposition* (the changing of a piece of music to another key). By simply starting the boogie woogie pattern from a different place on the fretboard, you can transpose the pattern to a new key. After you have mastered the whole piece in G, try it in other keys by going to any other fret and playing the same patterns.

In boogie woogie style, we usually use downstrokes only. When using a fast tempo, however, you may want to alternate between downstrokes and upstrokes.

Boogie woogie sounds great when one guitarist plays the boogie woogie pattern and another strums the chords (written above the staff) at the same time. On the recording, the strums are on one channel and the boogie woogie pattern is on the other. You can use the stereo's balance control to eliminate either part and play along.

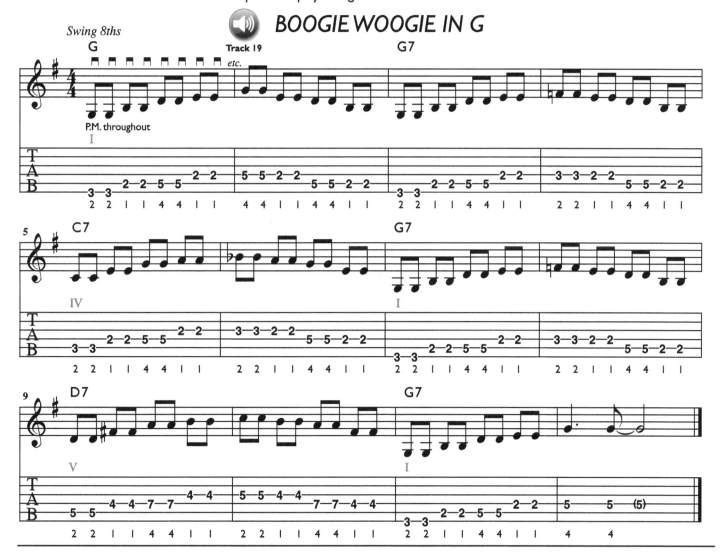

BOOGIE WOOGIE IN G

Track 19

The next piece is a boogie woogie in E, probably the most common guitar key for this style. The last two bars feature a popular *turnaround*. A turnaround comes at the end of a chorus and sets the music up to go back to the beginning or to end.

Notice in this piece that measures 1–8 are in the Easiest Blues form, and measures 9–12 are in the Most Common Blues form.

BOOGIE WOOGIE IN E

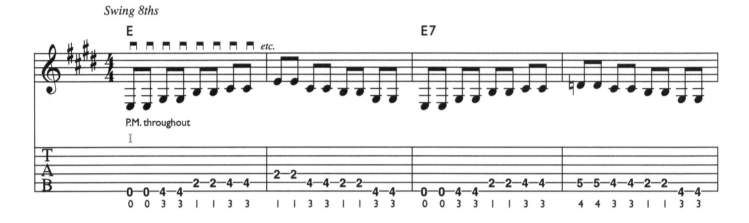

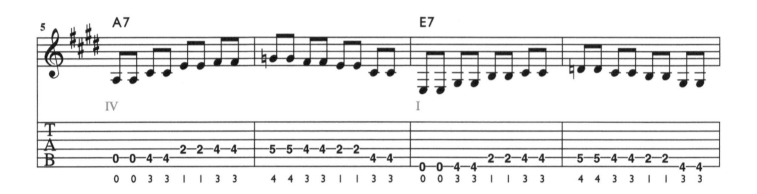

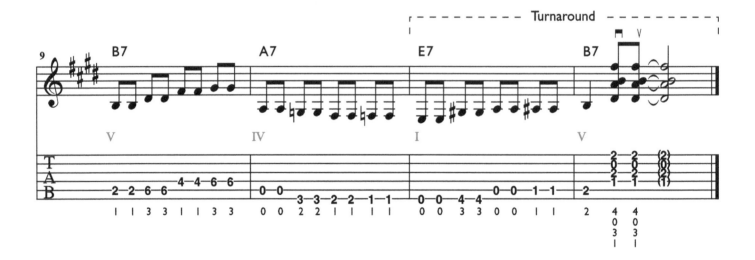

CHAPTER 9

Blues Strums

At a gig, a blues band may play the same progressions all night long. To keep the crowd interested, they will vary the keys and rhythms. The focus of this chapter is to teach you a variety of rhythmic patterns for blues rhythm guitar. They are exciting to play and will make your playing more interesting. We will apply these new strums to the standard 12-bar blues patterns you already know and will also introduce some new keys.

The following blues features an eighth-note strum and should be played in swing style. Remember, it is standard practice to use only downstrokes when playing two-string patterns, but when we strum full chords we usually alternate between downstrokes and upstrokes. The upstroke should be lighter than the downstroke—just hitting the first few strings, not the full chord. This gives our eighth notes the right blues bounce by accenting the first part of each beat (DA–da, DA–da, DA–da, DA–da). Use a pick at first, but later try strumming down with your thumb, and up with your index finger.

This following piece is in a new key: the key of C. The F7, the IV (see below), will probably be a new fingering for you. Practice it first and then tackle the following piece.

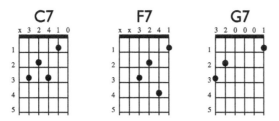

 12-BAR BLUES IN C

Track 21

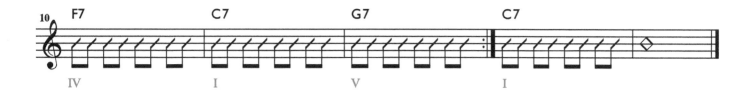

BLUES IN $\frac{12}{8}$

In $\frac{12}{8}$ time, there are 12 beats in a bar and each eighth note gets one beat. Potentially, there can be 12 eighth notes in each bar. However, you can think of the following strum as having four beats, with three equal eighth notes in each beat. The way to count in this time is: **1**–2–3, **2**–2–3, **3**–2–3, **4**–2–3, tapping your foot down on the 1, 2, 3 and 4.

To keep this rhythm interesting, it is important to accent beats 2 and 4 (see page 22, Backbeat).

This rhythm is often used in slow blues pieces.

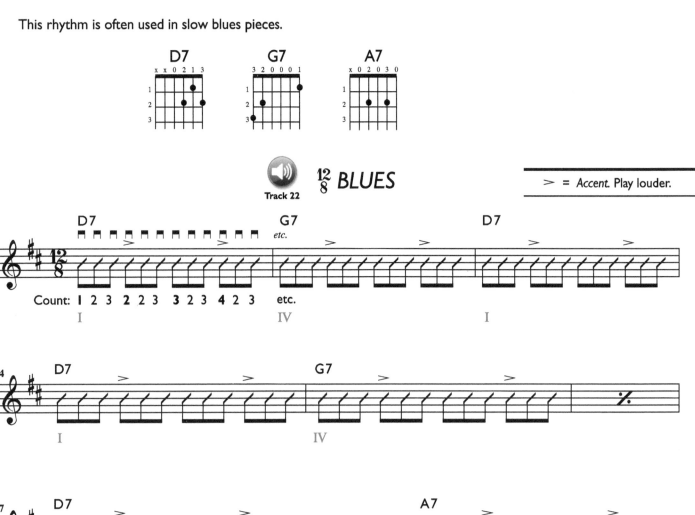

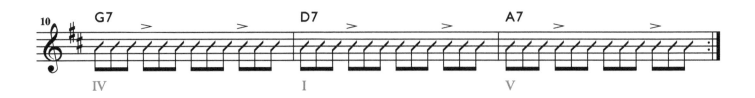

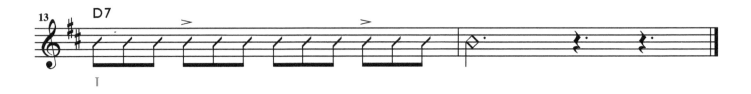

Our next example features one of the most common blues strums. It starts with a dotted quarter note on the first beat. Then there is an eighth note on the "&" of the 2nd beat which is tied to a half note. This gives us lots of "space," with only two strums in each bar. Both strums should be played with strong downstrokes. The placement of the second strum on the "&" of beat 2 creates *syncopation*, which is the shifting of emphasis from onbeats to offbeats (see page 13, Ties and Counting, for discussion of onbeats and offbeats).

When playing this rhythm, count: **1**–&, 2–**&**, 3–&,4–&, strumming down on the 1 and the "&" of beat 2. Be sure to count in swing style. Listen to the recording to make sure you are playing the rhythm correctly.

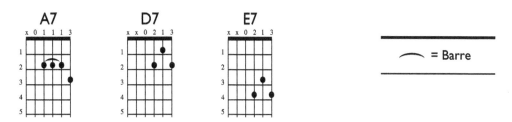

We are using a new chord form for A7. It is a partial *barre chord* (for a barre chord, one of your fingers must lie across two or more strings at the same fret). Lay your 1st finger across the 1st through 4th strings at the 2nd fret, while fretting the 3rd fret of the 1st string with your 3rd finger.

This E7 has the same fingering as D7, only moved two frets up. There is no E-note in this chord, which makes it a *rootless* chord. In blues, and especially jazz, rootless chords are not uncommon.

A7   D7   E7

⌢ = Barre

 TWO-STRUM BLUES IN A

Track 23

For our next piece, we've added a few more strums to the previous rhythm. Maintain the accents on beat 1 and the "&" of beat 2, strumming lighter for the rest of the measure. Be sure to strum downstrokes and upstrokes as indicated.

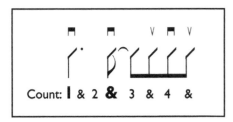

For the B7 chord, use the new A7 fingering, only two frets higher.

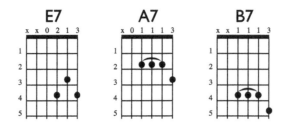

STRUMMIN' IN E

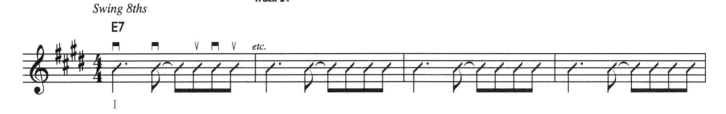

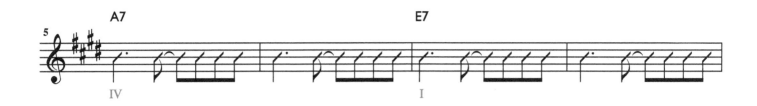

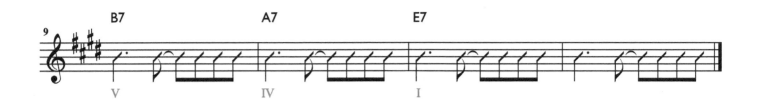

CHAPTER 10

Blues Soloing

Improvising (spontaneously creating) a good blues solo is an amazing experience. Once you know your scales and have acquired a feel for *phrasing* (the shaping of melodic lines), you'll soon be comfortable with this essential aspect of blues playing.

Learning to make up your own solos is critical. Even guitarists who play memorized solos, note-for-note, need to improvise to create their solos in the first place. Most players improvise different solos each time they play. They do, however, have a general idea of where they are "going" with their solo. Most players will also use classic *licks* in their improvisations. A lick is a short, standard phrase—part of the blues vocabulary that can be used by any player.

To be a good blues improviser, it is necessary to know the important blues scales, have a good repertoire of licks and have good phrasing. To become a real master takes a long time, but to play something simple that sounds good won't take long at all—if you practice, of course.

THE MINOR PENTATONIC SCALE

The *minor pentatonic scale* is one of the most common scales in blues, rock and other styles. A pentatonic scale has five notes. We'll compare the minor pentatonic scale to the major scale to understand its components. We'll do this in the key of E, since it is one of the most popular blues keys.

Here are the notes in an E Major scale:

The scale degrees of every minor pentatonic scale are: 1–♭3–4–5–♭7. An E Minor Pentatonic scale has the same 1st, 4th and 5th as the E Major scale (E, A and B). If we flat the G#, we get a G♮. G# is the 3rd note in the E major scale, so G♮ is considered the ♭3. Flatting the 7th, D#, gives us a D♮. The 2nd and 6th notes from the major scale are omitted. So, the notes of an E Minor Pentatonic scale are E–G–A–B–D.

You can use the formula (1–♭3–4–5–♭7) and your knowledge of major scales to determine the notes in any minor pentatonic scale.

Here is an E Minor Pentatonic scale in open position.

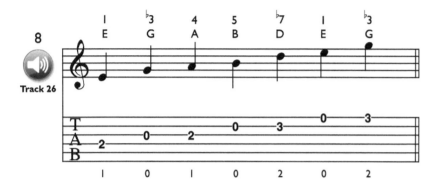

These dots tell us these open strings are part of the scale.

Numbers inside the dots are scale degrees.

E Minor Pentatonic Scale
(top four strings)

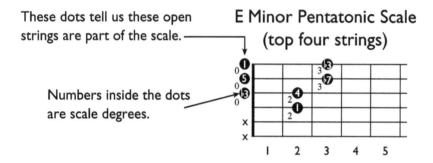

Practice all scales ascending and descending until you can play them with ease.

The following examples illustrate how parts of this scale are used to create blues phrases. Notice that they revolve around the 1, ♭3 and ♭7. These are the *target notes* (strongest or most characteristic notes) in this scale.

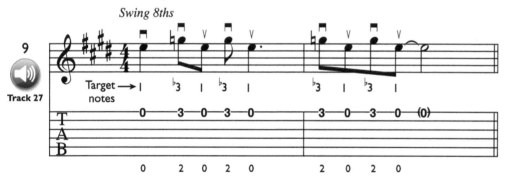

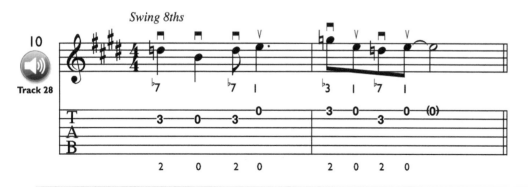

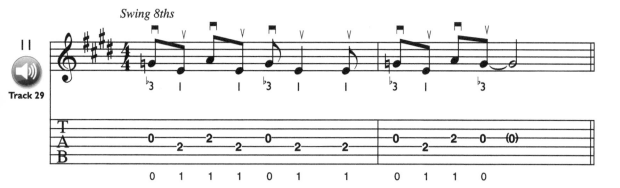

In this example, we extend the scale one note lower to a D♯ (the ♭7) on the 4th string.

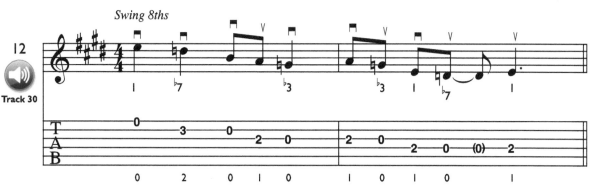

E Minor Pentatonic Scale (all six strings)

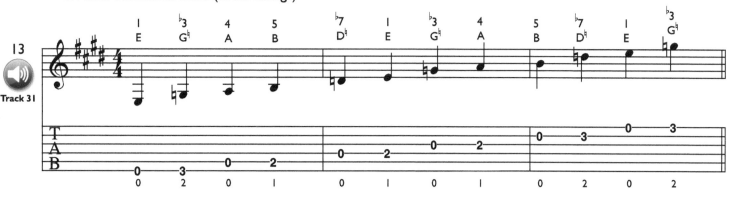

E Minor Pentatonic Scale (all six strings)

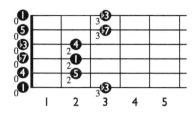

Here is a phrase using these lower notes.

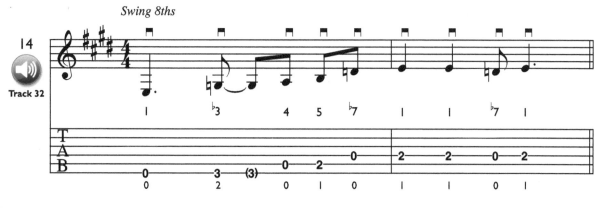

If we omit the 4 and 7 of the major scale, we create the *major pentatonic scale*. So, the scale degrees for the major pentatonic scale are 1–2–3–5–6. Like the minor pentatonic scale, it is one of the most popular scales used in the blues. It has a brighter sound than the minor pentatonic scale. Good target notes are the 1 and 3.

This fingering for the G Major Pentatonic scale has no open strings. It is a closed form (see page 43), which means it can be moved to different keys while maintaining the same fingering.

G Major Pentatonic Scale

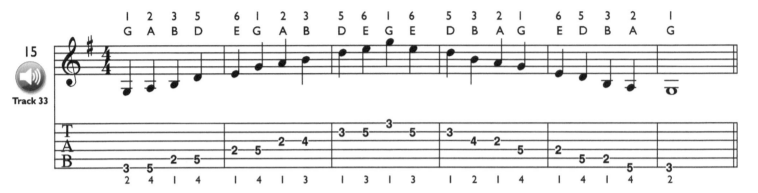

Major Pentatonic Scale (Moveable Form)

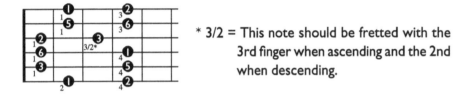

* 3/2 = This note should be fretted with the
3rd finger when ascending and the 2nd
when descending.

Here are two phrases made up of common, major pentatonic scale licks.

THE BLUES SCALE

There are a few widely used scales in blues, but only one is called the *blues scale*. This scale is identical to the minor pentatonic scale except for the addition of the ♭5. This is the note between the 4 and 5. We've seen that the ♭3 and ♭7 are altered notes that help to create the sound of the blues. The ♭5 goes even further in this bluesy direction. In fact, because it has such a strong and funky sound, it should be used sparingly. Normally, it is picked and then quickly resolved down to the 4—then down through the scale to the 1. It also sounds good when resolved up to the 5. The blues scale has the same target notes as the minor pentatonic scale: 1, ♭3 and ♭7. Although you don't want to overdo it, you should also target the ♭5—just enough to bring out its distinctive color.

Memorize where the ♭5s are in the following E Blues scale fingering.

E Blues Scale

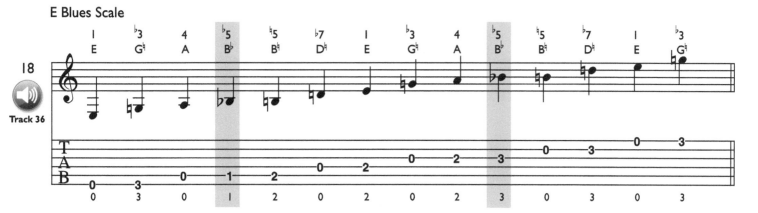

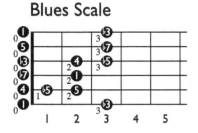

The following phrases will show you common ways to incorporate the ♭5 into your playing.

MOVEABLE SCALE FORMS

Below are moveable versions of the minor and major pentatonic scales and the blues scale. Since they do not use open strings, they can be moved up or down the neck to any key. To do this, just move the scale to the position where the letter name of the I corresponds to the letter name of the key in which you want to play. Then start improvising, using the phrases of the preceding pages as a springboard for your own ideas.

You need to know each of the fingerings on this page; they are the most common scale forms used in the blues.

Minor Pentatonic Scale

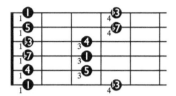

Blues Scale

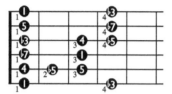

Major Pentatonic Scale

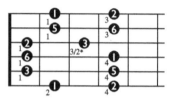

* 3rd finger ascending
2nd finger descending

Minor Pentatonic with Upper Extension
(ascending fingering)

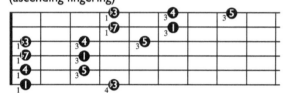

Minor Pentatonic with Upper Extension
(descending fingering)

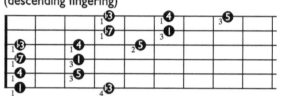

Blues Scale
(ascending fingering)

Blues Scale
(descending fingering)

Scale Tips

Here are some tips to help you eventually play faster and get a fuller sound.

- Hold previously fretted notes down as you play higher notes on the same string. This sustains the lower note until the higher note is sounded.

- When moving up or down from one string to another, don't lift your fingers too soon. The finger fretting the last note on a string should stay in place as another finger moves to the next note on the next string. This creates a slight overlap and gives us continuous sound, without gaps between notes.

- Make up your own blues phrases. Try to copy the examples from this chapter using the moveable scale forms.

- Practice each scale fingering—ascending and descending—until you can play them in your sleep. Then wake up and use them when playing with other players or along with albums.

Have fun improvising.

PHRASING

The motto in real estate may be "location, location, location," but in blues soloing it's "phrasing, phrasing, phrasing." Phrasing is how we put notes together to make musical statements. As you play more and more, your phrasing will improve. Listen to the phrasing of great blues artists like B.B. King. Stay focused when you solo. You really need to be "in the moment" to make interesting musical choices with the notes and rhythms you play.

PHRASING TIPS

- **Do not play too many notes.**
  You don't need to use every note in the scale for every solo. Develop licks that you can play on one or two strings. You can make a great solo with only one or two notes if you use cool rhythms. Someone once said that if you play a lot of notes, it will sound like you're looking for the right one.

- **Phrases should revolve around target notes.**
  Remember that each scale has target notes that are used more than other notes in the scale. The 1, or tonic, is the most important note in any key; it's a good beginning and ending note for phrases. The $\flat 3$, $\flat 5$ and $\flat 7$ are colorful notes that help to create the blues sound. In a major key, target notes are the 1 and $\natural 3$. Be sure, though, not to start and end each phrase with one of these notes. Use others for interest and variety. The tonic is *stable*, which means it does not need to be resolved to any other note, but ending on another note can create suspense and "leave you hanging."

- **Repeat melodic fragments and full phrases.**
  You don't need a lot of different ideas for a solo. Repetition allows the listener to more fully absorb good phrases or statements. To add variety, try repeating phrases, but on different beats in a measure.

- **Add color and excitement by regularly using expressive techniques** such as hammer-ons, pull-offs, slides, bends and vibrato (all covered in the next chapter, Left-Hand Techniques, page 56).

- **Create "space" in your solos.**
  Beginners often try to fill every moment with notes, but this will sound too busy. Add space between your phrases to let the audience absorb the music. A long pause can create tension and will add more excitement to the next phrase.

- **Add interest by varying your rhythms.**
  Eighth notes are the most common rhythmic value in blues soloing, but use longer and shorter values for variety.

- **Listen to recorded solos that move you and imitate them.**
  Try to copy the licks and phrases, or at least copy the rhythms to create your own musical statements.

- **Express yourself.**
  Focus on the emotion you want to convey and put it into your playing.

CHAPTER 11

Left-Hand Techniques

In this chapter, we will cover techniques that are absolutely vital for blues players. All of them, except one, are *legato* techniques. On the guitar, they are produced when we pick one note and sound other notes with our left hand. Practice all of the examples until they become comfortable. Then try to incorporate them into your soloing.

HAMMER-ONS

To play a *hammer-on,* pick one note and sound the next note on the same string by "hammering-on" with a left-hand finger. The second note is not picked. To do this effectively, you need to bring your left-hand finger down cleanly on the fret, just behind the fret wire. Think of tapping the note with your left-hand finger, rather than just fretting it. In a good hammer-on, each note will be equal in volume. A curved line ⌒ called a slur, connecting one note to a higher note, indicates a hammer-on.

The following example shows the E Minor Pentatonic scale played with hammer-ons.

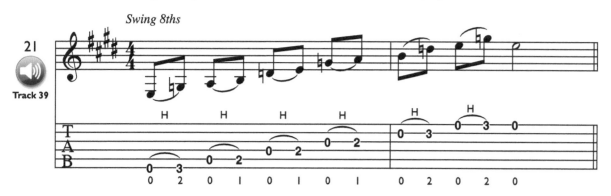

This phrase starts with a common hammer-on lick.

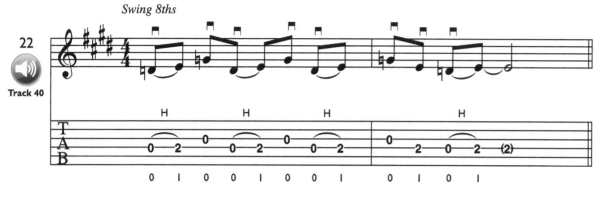

PULL-OFFS

A slur connecting one note to a lower note indicates a *pull-off*. This technique is accomplished by picking a fretted note, then "pulling-off" with the left-hand finger that is fretting the note. This activates a lower note on the same string. The second note can be open or fretted. If it's a fretted note, your finger must be in place ahead of time, before the pull-off is set into motion. With a little practice, both notes should be equal in volume. Keep in mind that you cannot pull-off from an open string.

A more appropriate name for pull-offs would be "pull-downs," because a downward motion (toward the floor) is needed for a strong second note. As a demonstration of this, put a left-hand finger on a note and, without picking the string, lift your finger horizontally off the string. You'll notice that a very quiet sound is produced. Now fret the same note again. Do not pick the string, but move your finger downward, staying in contact with the fretboard. Flick the string as your finger moves down. The lower note should ring clearly and your finger should come to rest against the next string (if you pull-off on the 1st string, your finger would wind up just off the neck). By doing this, you will have two strong notes. At first, you may sound unwanted open strings when you pull-off. If this occurs, practice muting the open strings with the sides of your left-hand fingers or right-hand palm.

Here is a descending E Minor Pentatonic scale played with pull-offs.

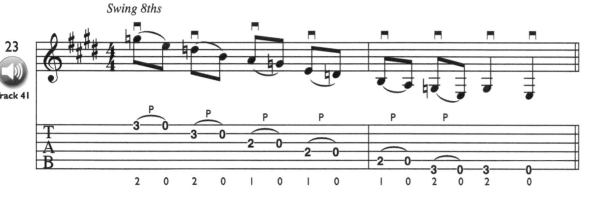

The pull-offs in this phrase are common in blues soloing.

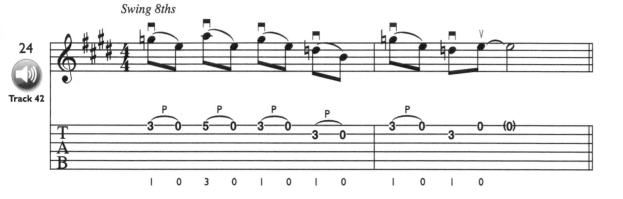

BENDING

The *bend* is one of the most expressive techniques in the blues and it is often used to imitate the phrasing of the human voice. To bend, play a fretted note and bend—or push—the string to get the pitch of another note.

When bending, we need to have a "destination" note in mind. We push the string until we get the sound of a second note. This second note is almost always another note in the scale; we bend from one scale-note to the pitch of another. At first, your destination note may sound out of tune; you may be bending too far or not far enough to get an accurate pitch on the second note. When practicing bends, play your destination note first and get the sound of it in your mind. Then practice bending to that sound. You can also use an electronic tuner to help you practice bending to the correct note.

In acoustic blues, we use half-step and whole-step bends. Bending works best on the first two strings because they are the thinnest. It is also easier to bend in the middle of the neck, where the strings are looser and have more "give." In TAB and standard music notation, bends are indicated by a curved arrow. The number above the arrow tells us if it is a half- or whole-step bend.

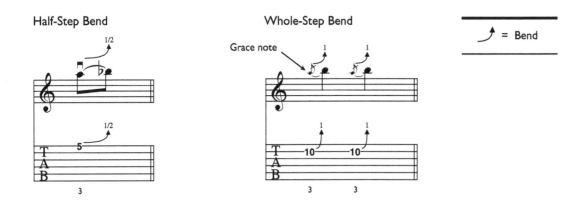

Aside from the distance of the bend (half or whole step), there other differences between bends. In one case, we let the first note ring for a full rhythmic value (see illustration for half-step bend above). In another case, we pick a note and bend so fast that we do not let the first note ring out. This is actually a way of playing the second note; it is an *embellishment.* In this type of bend, the first note is called a *grace note.* In standard music notation, a grace note is written as a tiny eighth-note ♪, but in TAB, it is written the same way as any other note. So if you're reading the tablature, make sure you look at the standard music notation to see if a note is a grace note or not.

Learn to bend notes with more than one finger. For example, when bending the 5th fret on the 1st string, use your 3rd finger on the 5th fret, but also place your 2nd finger on the 4th fret, and your 1st finger on the 3rd fret. This is the secret to better bending. It gives you more strength and control. Sometimes, though, we *do* bend with the 1st finger alone—so this also must be practiced. In fact, it's a good idea to practice bending with every finger. For most bends, you will be pushing the string up toward the ceiling, but for those on the 5th and 6th strings, you will pull the string down toward the floor.

Learn the common bend-notes in each scale: the 4 and ♭7 in the minor pentatonic and blues scales, and the 2 in the major pentatonic scale.

Here are a couple of simple phrases that use bends.

PRE-BENDS AND REVERSE BENDS

This next example demonstrates the *reverse bend*. Here, we *pre-bend* a note before striking it. Bend first, then pick the string and release the bend. It's a great technique, but be sure to keep the finger pressure on the note or it will die out.

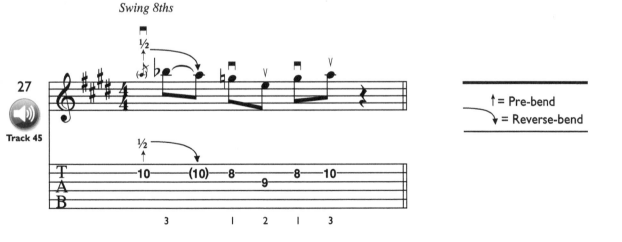

↑ = Pre-bend

↓ = Reverse-bend

SLIDES

A *slide* is accomplished by picking one fretted note and, keeping finger pressure on the string, sliding to a second note on the same string. Slides can be played ascending and descending.

There are three kinds of slides: *measured, grace-note* and *unspecified*. In a measured slide, the first note rings for a full rhythmic value. In a grace-note slide, we pick a note and quickly slide to the next, not allowing the first to sustain at all. In this type of slide, the first note is a grace note. In an unspecified slide, in which a starting location is not given, you can usually start a whole or half step below the destination note.

A slide is indicated by a straight line between two notes.

Measured Slide

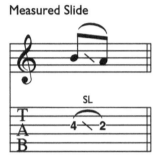

Grace-Note Slide

Unspecified Slide

The following phrase uses grace-note slides on the upper three strings.

Below, we are sliding to notes on the 2nd string while playing the open 1st string. In the first bar, the E on the 2nd string and the E on the 1st string are *unisons*. In this example, we are using unspecified slides. In the 1st measure, you can start from the 3rd fret and slide up to the 5th fret. However, in the next measure, it would make sense to start from the 5th fret (because you are already there) and slide up to the 8th fret. Experiment. See what sounds best to you.

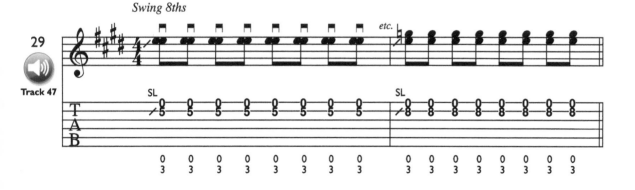

This left-hand technique is *not* a slur. *Vibrato* is a series of quick, tiny bends and is often used on the last notes and other longer notes in blues phrases. Listen to all of the great blues players and singers and you will hear a distinct fluctuation of pitch on their ending notes. This adds liveliness and sustain to a note.

To use this technique, play a fretted note anywhere on the neck. Pretend to "itch" the note after you pick it, by moving your finger slightly up and down. Be sure to keep pressure on the note and you will hear the pitch fluctuate. Try to keep this fluctuation even. Vibrato can be fast or slow depending upon the speed of your movement. It can also be wide or narrow depending on how far the finger moves from its starting spot. Most players shoot for a narrow vibrato of moderate speed. Listen to your favorite artists to check out their approach. Learn to automatically apply vibrato to your longer notes.

Vibrato is indicated by a wavy line.

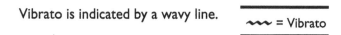

Try the following examples using vibrato.

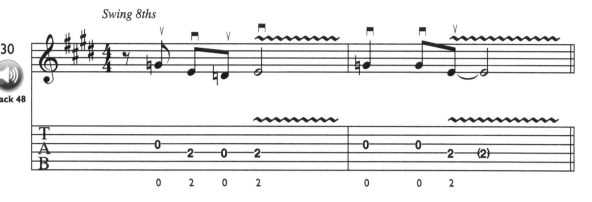

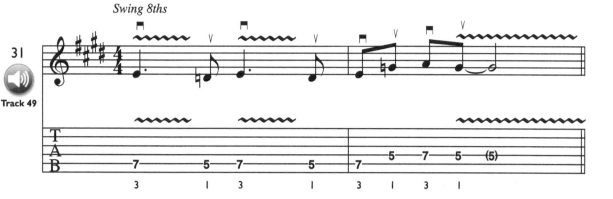

A good player will combine the techniques covered in this chapter, using some more than others. This is part of what makes their individual style.

The following phrases combine the techniques covered in this chapter.

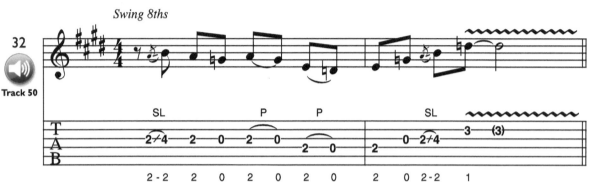

Watch out for the consecutive pull-offs in the 1st measure. Your 1st finger must be in place on the 3rd fret before you start the pull-off on the 5th fret.

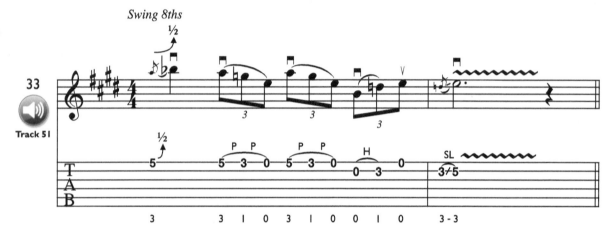

CHAPTER 12

More Blues Strums and Right-Hand Patterns

To the right are the chords you will need in the following examples.

The voicing for B♭7 is a new one for you. It's very common and has a great sound. E♭7 and F7 have the same shape as the C7 chord we learned on page 25, but here we move it up the neck to other positions. There are no open strings in these chords; this makes them *closed voicings*. Be sure to mute the strings that are not part of these chords. Do this by touching them with the sides of the fingers that are fretting notes, or by using other parts of your left hand. This is tricky at first, but you'll get used to it in time. In this book, hollow dots indicate the roots of all chords with closed voicings.

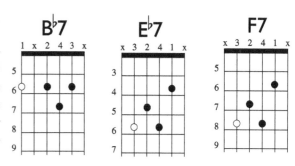

The first new strum we will try is similar to the one we learned on page 47. In both strums, we strike the strings in the same rhythm, but there is an important difference. In the earlier strum we extended the note values with ties. Here we will cut each strum short with rests.

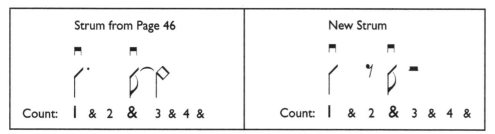

We want a percussive and choppy sound. This style is easy to achieve with closed voicings. After each strum, immediately lift your left-hand fingers—just slightly—to stop the strings from vibrating. Do not lift off the strings completely—just enough to stop the chord from ringing. With open string chords, this is more difficult. The chord must be silenced by quickly touching the strings with the side of your picking hand.

The key of B♭ is often used in jazz-blues, or when playing with sax or brass players.

B♭ BLUES
Track 52

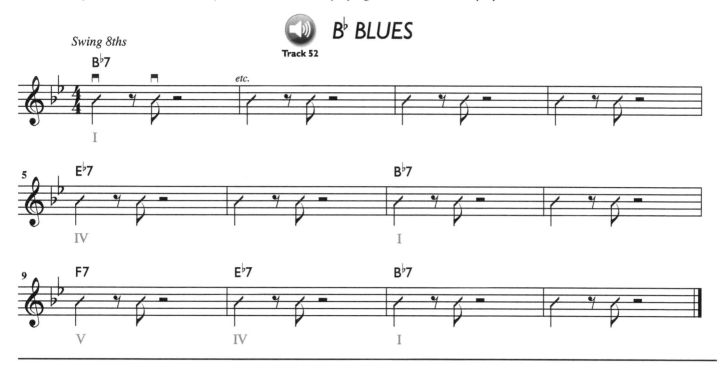

Arpeggios are the notes of a chord played one at a time. This produces a lighter texture than strumming full chords. Arpeggios can be played using any combination of strings, but the string pattern for our example is 4th–3rd–2nd–1st–2nd–3rd, etc.

You can use a pick or you can try it fingerstyle. When playing fingerstyle, use your thumb for the 4th string, your index finger for the 3rd string, your middle finger for the 2nd string and your ring finger on the 1st string.

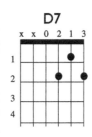
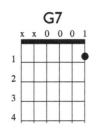
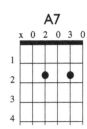

ARPEGGION BLUES

Track 53

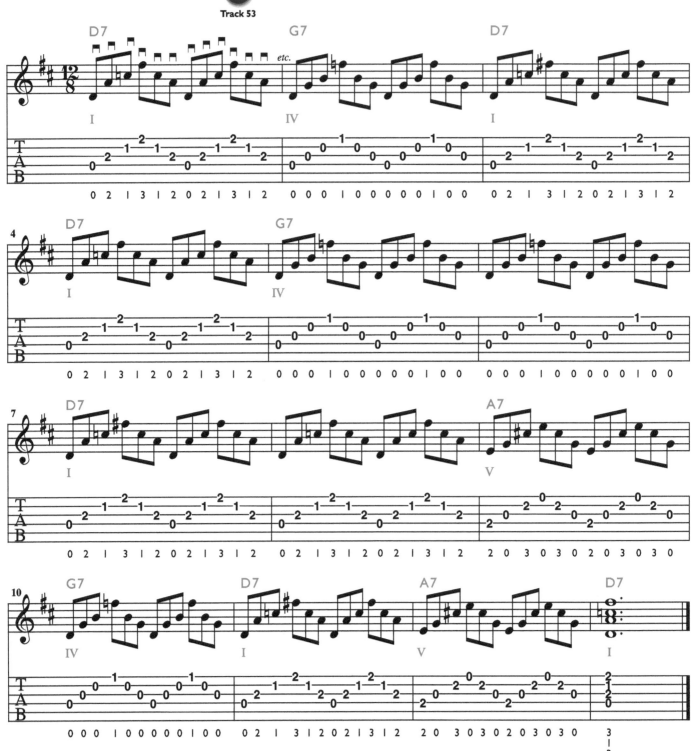

THE SIXTEENTH-NOTE STRUM

Our next rhythm is made up entirely of sixteenth notes. Remember, the duration of a sixteenth note is a quarter of a beat. They are counted: "1–e–&–ah, 2–e–&–ah, etc."

In our next piece, there will be four sixteenth notes for every beat in each measure. If we were to play a measure of eighth notes, and then a measure of sixteenth notes at the same tempo, the sixteenth notes would sound twice as fast as the eighth notes.

Strums like this are more common in funk guitar, but blues can be funky too. Keep your right hand and arm loose and steady. Be sure to accent the first sixteenth note of each set of four. Rhythms like this are often played with *9 chords*. The scale degrees that make up a 9 chord are 1–3–5–♭7–9. In this tune, the IV and V are 9 chords.

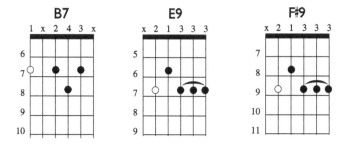

FUNKY BLUES IN B

Track 54

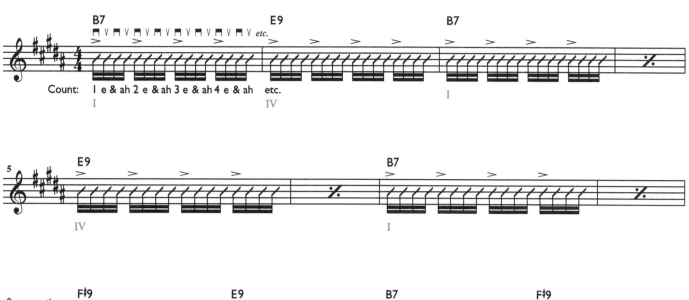

At fast tempos, players will sometimes use a strum that consists of only upstrokes played on the offbeats (&s). These are usually played with a short, choppy feel. On the acoustic guitar, it sounds great if you tap the strings with your right hand on the onbeats. The sound you are looking for is that of your hand lightly hitting the body, along with the metallic sound the strings make as they tap the frets on the neck. It's a great percussive sound. This type of strum is also used in "ska" music.

On the onbeats, tap the strings with your right hand. This is represented by × in the song below.

On the offbeats, strum up.

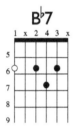

 ## UPBEAT BLUES IN F

Track 55

× = Unpitched, percussive sound.

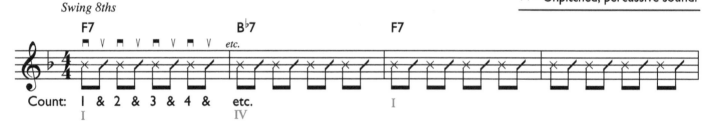

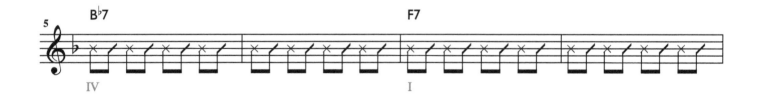

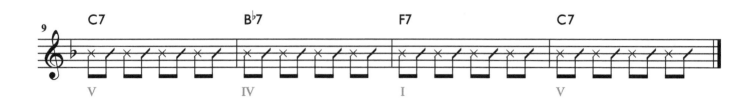

CHAPTER 13

Turnarounds

Although many players call the last *four* bars of a blues form the *turnaround,* this term more often refers to a melodic phrase played in the last *two* bars. There are many classic turnarounds that are played over and over again at gigs or jams. They are really fun to play and serve as a signal to other musicians (and to the audience) that a chorus is over and another will be played. As a blues player, it's essential to know the classic turnarounds as they are an integral part of the blues vocabulary.

The examples that follow are all standard turnarounds. They are written in the popular keys of E and A, but eventually, you should learn them in other common keys. Practice them a bit. There will be more information on how to use them at the end of this chapter.

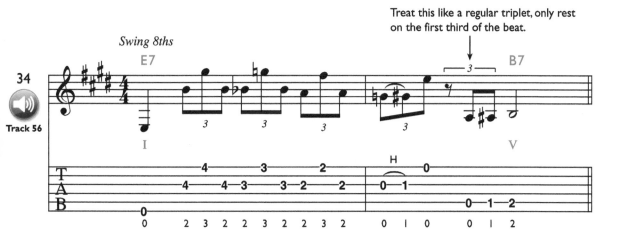

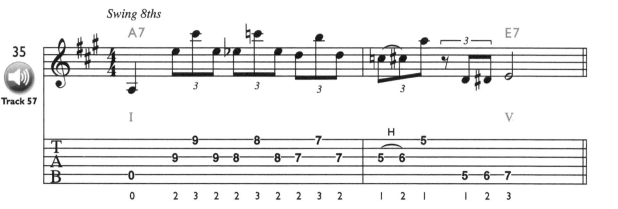

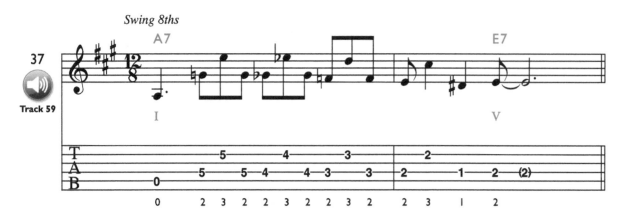

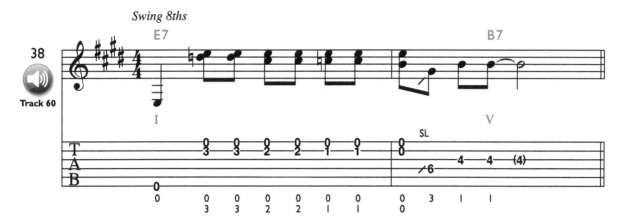

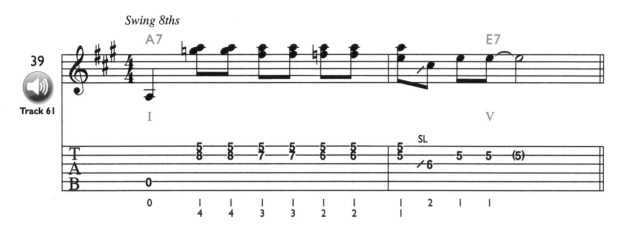

The above turnaround (example 42) is fairly simple. See if you can transpose it yourself and play it in the key of A. You might want to review page 43 (Closed Forms) for an explanation of transposition. Even though there are open strings in this turnaround, it can be transposed to the key of A very easily. Instead of playing the note pattern on the 6th and 5th strings, play it on the 5th and 4th strings. To see how you did, see below.

Example 42—Transposed to the Key of A

Below is a turnaround consisting entirely of chords; first in E, then in A. Be sure to use the fingerings in the chord diagrams above the staff.

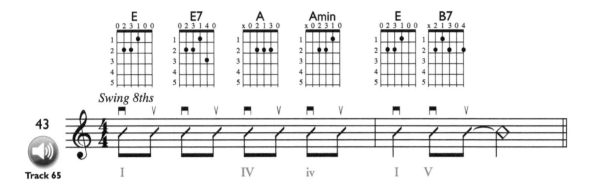

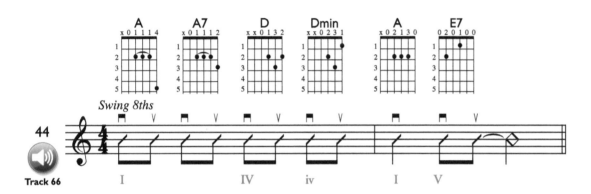

Notice that all the turnarounds are two bars long. Although almost every example begins with a low E or A root-note, the distinctive phrase of each turnaround starts on the second beat.

You can use these classic turnarounds, in the appropriate key, in any piece you play. Play through your chord progression and merely substitute the turnaround for the last two bars. This will work in any of the blues forms you have learned. You can leave the first beat of the turnaround silent; you can strum a I chord in a strumming piece; you can hit a quarter-note 5th if you're playing a shuffle; or just go ahead and play that low root.

Pick your favorite examples and add them to progressions you've learned in this book, and also to any songs you may learn in the future.

You can also use a turnaround as an intro to a piece. It's done often and is an exciting way to kick off a blues tune.

Finally, all the turnarounds in this book can be used as endings if you change the final chord from a V to a I.

CHAPTER 14

Riff Style Blues

A *riff* is a short, repeated phrase that is usually played on the lower strings. Many blues pieces are based on riffs. This riff is moved to different starting notes that correspond to the root-notes of the I, IV and V chords of the key.

Our first riff piece is a *minor blues* (a blues progression in which most or all of the chords are minor chords) in the style of the famous tunes, "Help Me," by Sonny Boy Williamson and "Green Onions," by Booker T. & the MG's. We'll take another look at the minor blues in a later chapter (page 83, Minor Blues).

Notice the last three measures. Here you will see *1st* and *2nd endings*. Play through the piece until you come to the 1st repeat sign. Go back and play from the beginning. When you come to the 1st ending, do not play it, but skip over to the 2nd ending and play to the end. Remember to use your balance control to play along with either the chords or the riff on the recording.

RIFF BLUES IN E MINOR

Track 67

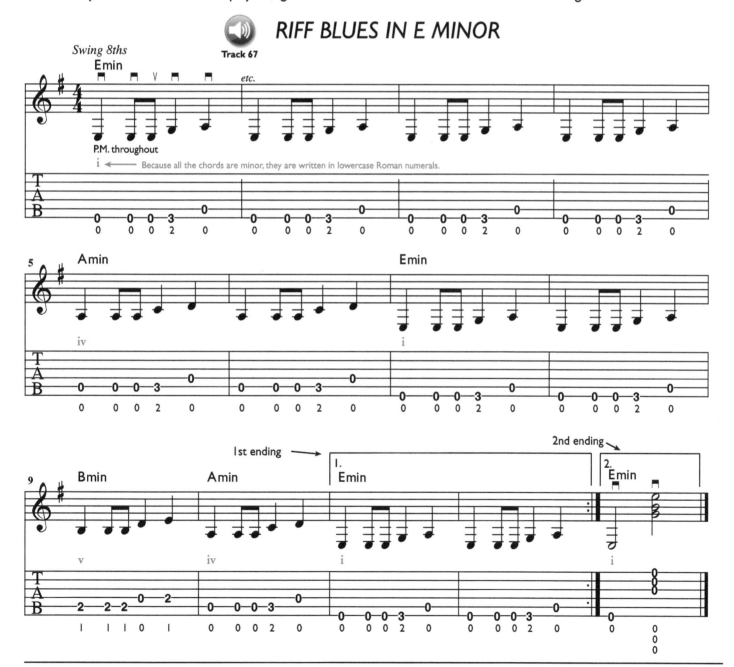

The riff piece below is in the key of F and based on a boogie woogie pattern. For rhythmic variety, there is a triplet on the fourth beat of each measure. The piece also has a popular ending in which a 9 chord built on the $\flat$6 (D$\flat$) moves a half step down to a 9 chord built on the 5 (C). This ending even appears in some Elvis songs!

RIFFIN' IN F

Track 68

Our next riff blues starts with an octave jump.

OCTAVE BLUES

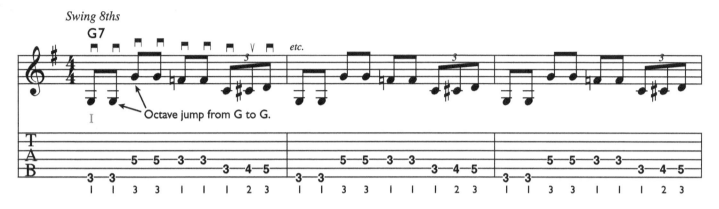

Octave jump from G to G.

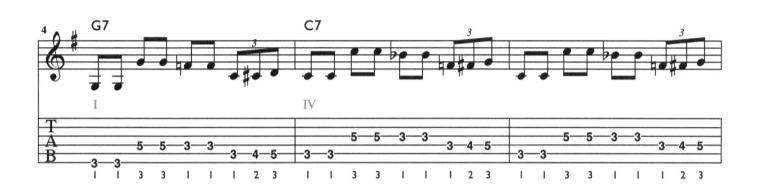

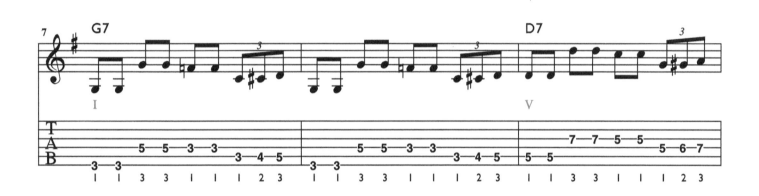

This straight eighth-note piece is a minor blues with a funky sound. Minor 7 chords are incorporated in the riff. The first appearance of the v (notice the lowercase Roman numeral) chord in bar 9 is as a D Minor 7, but in the last bar, the v becomes a V and appears as a D7#9. The dominant 7#9 produces another colorful blues sound. It is also used often in funk and rock. Jimi Hendrix used it in "Purple Haze" and other songs. In fact, some people refer to the 7#9 as "the Hendrix chord."

FUNKY BLUES IN G MINOR

Track 70

CHAPTER 15

Moveable Two-String Patterns

In Chapter 4 (pages 27–28), we discussed shuffles that were based on alternating perfect 5ths and major 6ths. Each of those patterns were based on open-string root-notes. In this section, we will see how we can transpose these sounds to fretted roots. This will allow us to play in the shuffle style in any key.

The following "5" and "6" shapes have their roots on the 6th and 5th strings and are in the key of G. In the key of G, the I chord is G, the IV chord is C and the V chord is D.

Root-6 Shapes
(root on the 6th string)

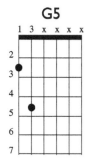

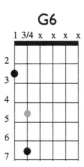

Root-5 Shapes
(root on the 5th string)

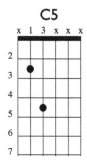

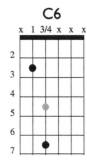

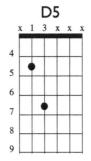

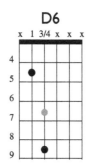

It's easy to change keys using the shapes on this page. If you use the root-6 shape as the I chord—anywhere on the neck—the IV will always be a root-5 shape on the same fret. If you move the IV chord two frets higher, you get the V.

The shuffle below is in the key of G. The turnaround is based on a dominant 7, three-note fingering that descends in half steps. This is followed by a 9 chord built on the ♭6 (E♭9) that moves to a 9 chord built on the 5 (D9).

This piece does not include the move to the ♭7 (see page 31). Some people, especially those with smaller hands, have trouble stretching to this colorful note. Try adding it in if you can. It's always one fret higher than the 6. If you can't reach it yet, practice stretching with your 4th finger and you will get it eventually.

SHUFFLE IN G

Track 71

Now we will use our moveable two-string shapes to play a piece with straight eighth notes. It's in the key of B♭ and in the style of Chuck Berry's "Johnny B. Goode." Some of Jimmy Reed's famous songs are also in this rockin' blues, straight eighth-note style.

CHUCK'S BLUES

Track 72

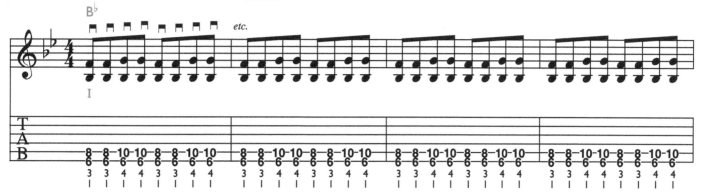

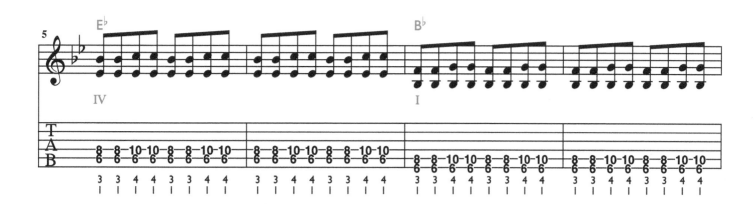

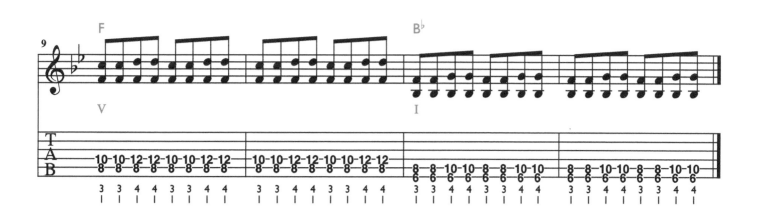

Sometimes the notes of these two-string patterns are played separately. This technique is used in the Most Common Blues in E below. Notice there is a note before the first full measure of music. This is a *pickup*. Count one full measure of four beats, then come in with the pickup on the "&" of beat 4. Theoretically, the missing beats of the pickup measure come from the beats of the last measure, which is incomplete.

SHUFFLIN' IN E

Track 73

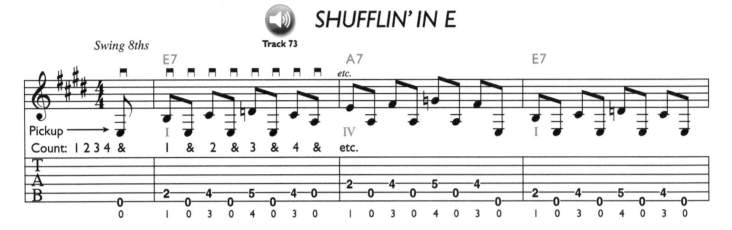

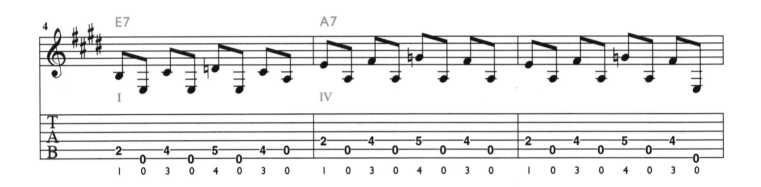

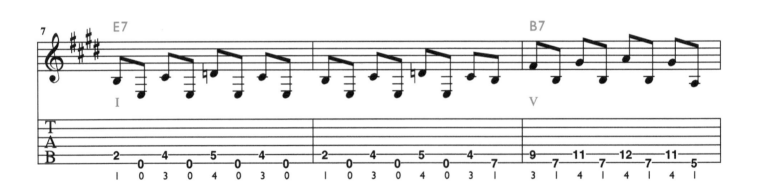

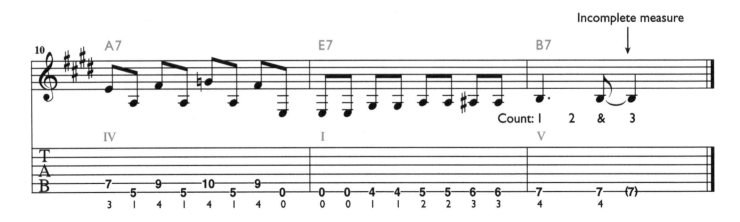

CHAPTER 16

Barre Chords

Barre chords, first introduced on page 47, are an essential tool for a guitarist. Remember, these are chords in which one finger, usually the 1st, lies flat over a fret and presses multiple strings. They are used in blues and almost every other guitar style. They are moveable shapes—closed voicings—that can be played on any fret. They can be a little tricky to play correctly but they will have to be mastered.

Start working on these only when you are comfortable with the other chords in this book. At that point, your left-hand fingers will have the strength and agility needed to play barre chords.

Below are all the important barre chord shapes. Practice each shape on various frets up and down the neck. Listen to each note in the chord and adjust your fingers to get a clear sound from each.

A barre is indicated with a curved line ———— over the strings to be barred. Remember, hollow dots indicate the roots of the chords.

Root-6 Barre Chords

Major	Minor	7	Minor 7
1 3 4 2 1 1	1 3 4 1 1 1	1 3 1 2 1 1	1 3 1 1 1 1

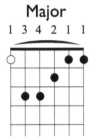 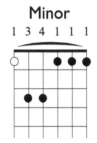 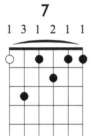 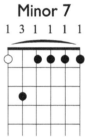

Root-5 Barre Chords

Major	Minor	7	Minor 7
x 1 3 3 3 x	x 1 3 4 2 1	x 1 3 1 4 1	x 1 3 1 2 1

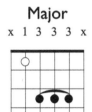 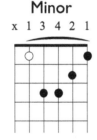 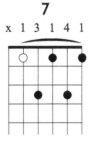 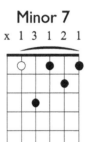

This piece is in the key of A♭, but you should try it in other keys as well. Take note, there are two different fingerings for A♭7. They are numbered ① and ② so you know which to use.

You will be using dominant 7 barre chords, but it is a good idea to practice blues progressions using major, minor and minor 7 barre chords as well. Start with a root-6 I chord, and the IV will always be a root-5 shape on the same fret. The V will always be two frets higher than the IV.

Here are the chords you will need for this progression.

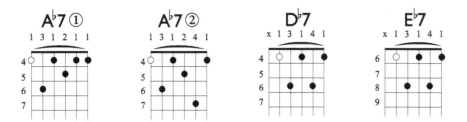

 A♭ BARRE BLUES

Track 74

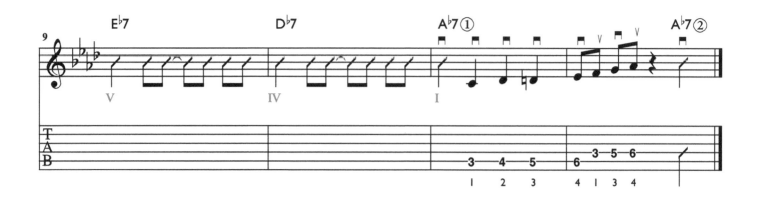

CHAPTER 17

Eight-Bar Blues

Although the 12-bar pattern is by far the most popular blues form, the *eight-bar blues* is also fairly common. This is a blues form made up of eight measures.

This following tune is in the style of "Key to the Highway," a blues classic by Bill Broonzy that has been recorded by many artists.

The triplet on the fourth beat of each measure adds rhythmic variety to our piece.

KEY TO THE TURNPIKE

Track 75

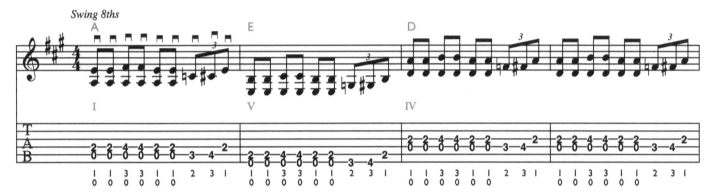

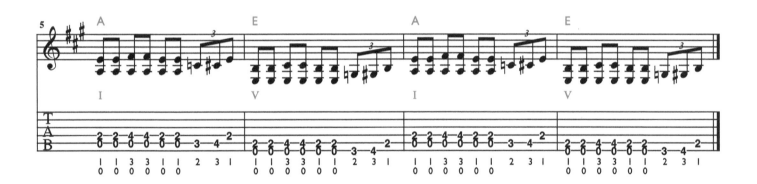

"How Long Blues" was a huge hit for the influential duo of Leroy Carr and Scrapper Blackwell in 1928. It is a standard, or a "must know" tune for any blues player. This next song is in the style of "How Long Blues," but is based on a version of the song by Leadbelly.

Leadbelly was a Texas musician who led a colorful life. He had a very strong guitar sound. Known as the "King of the 12-String Guitar," he strummed down on the lower strings with his thumb, and up on the upper strings with his fingers, or index finger. Try this approach with the next piece. When it's comfortable for you, try it with other songs too. It's a great technique for creating a slightly rough, down-home sound.

Notice there are two different fingerings for the E7 chord.

TOO LONG BLUES

Track 76

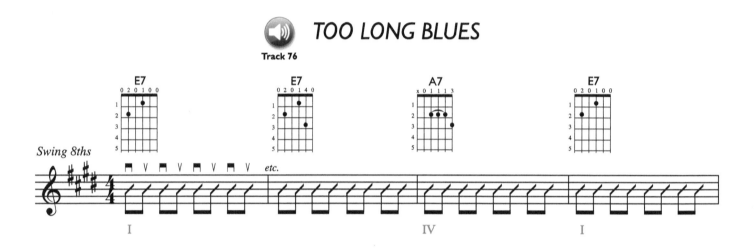

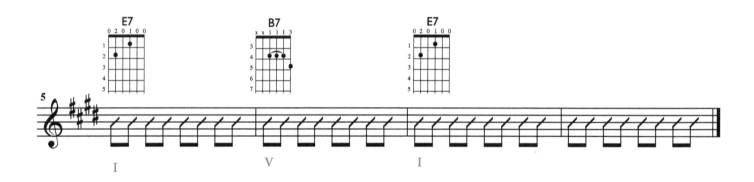

CHAPTER 18

Minor Blues

Remember, a *minor blues* is a progression in which most or all of the chords are minor chords. As you may have noticed in the minor blues pieces we have already played (pages 71 and 74), they have a very distinct sound and are a great alternative to the major and dominant 7 sound we get from most other blues. Some would say they give us a deeper, moodier and more soulful sound.

The following progression is composed entirely of minor chords. The i chord is Amin; the iv chord is Dmin; the v chord is Emin.

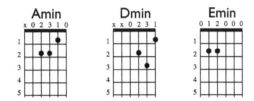

 MINOR BLUES IN A
Track 77

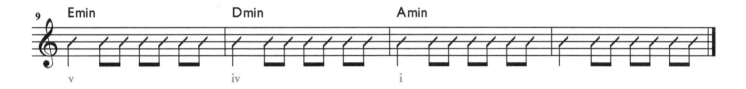

Although it will be more difficult, you can try the above minor blues with the barre chords below.

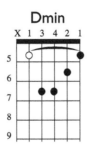

Though in our last piece we used Emin, it is standard practice in minor blues to make the v a dominant 7 chord. This would make the Emin an E7. Our next piece uses this approach.

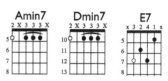

Minor 7 chords are used instead of the straight minor chords. When you play the chord voicings in this piece, be sure to mute any open strings. Remember, this is done by lightly touching them with the fingers that are fretting notes on adjacent strings. The strum for this piece is similar to the strum you learned on page 63, with the exception that there is a quarter-note strum on the last beat of each measure.

THREE-STRUM BLUES

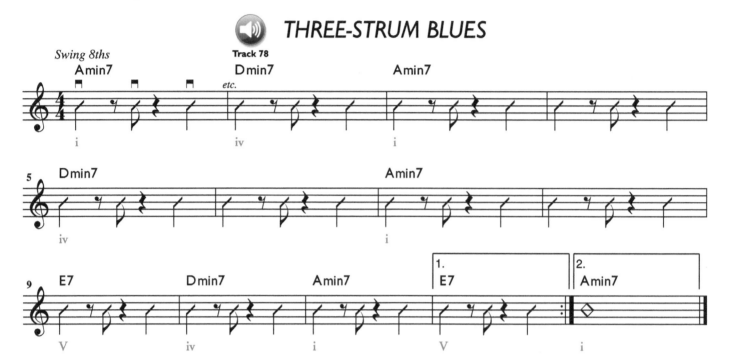

This next progression is in the style of B. B. King's "The Thrill Is Gone." It has minor 7 chords and even a G Major 7 chord (which is a ♭VI). The Bmin7 and F♯7 will sound best with the barre chord voicings to the right. However, if these chords are too difficult for you at this point, you can use the alternative chords next to them.

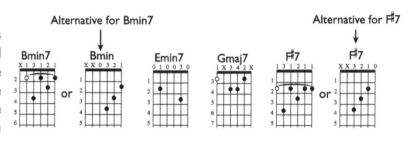

BLUES FOR B. B.

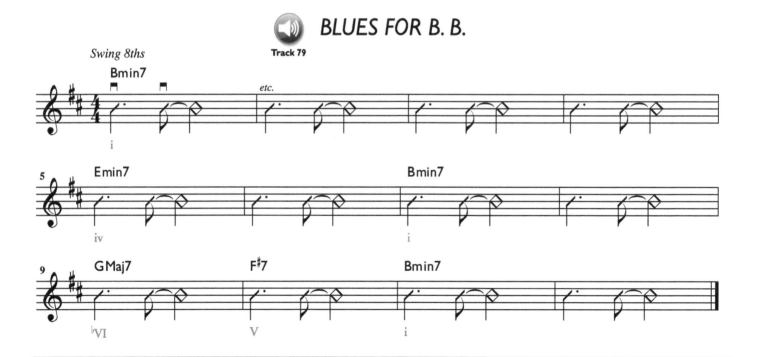

CHAPTER 19

Fingerstyle Blues

In this chapter, the basics of fingerstyle blues technique will be introduced. All the early pioneers of the blues were fingerstyle players. Playing fingerstyle is a fun and rewarding way to play.

Let's start by talking about the right hand. It's traditional to use Spanish terms for the right-hand fingers, and these are then abbreviated:

- *pulgar (p)* for thumb
- *indice (i)* for index
- *medio (m)* for middle
- *anular (a)* for ring

Your index *(i)*, middle *(m)* and ring *(a)* fingers are assigned to the upper three strings. Your thumb should cover the notes on the lower three strings. In standard music notation, notes played with the thumb are written with the stems going down. This is the rule for all the pieces in this chapter, and is the general approach for most fingerstyle playing.

Most fingerstyle blues pieces are based on chords. A chord is held with the left hand and the right hand picks notes from it in various rhythms. The notes from these chords need to be held; they should continue to ring out even after they are plucked. This is important because you will see individual notes in the music. Do not try to play the pieces by jumping from one individual note to another. Instead, hold the correct chord for that measure, and all the notes you need will be there. In more melodic pieces, like "Blues for Mississippi John" (page 88), the upper notes cannot be held, but be sure to let the bass notes sustain. In general, holding notes as long as possible (especially the notes played by the thumb) will give you a full sound.

When practicing, it's a good idea to repeat each bar a few times. This will get the phrases under your fingers and help you master the piece.

MINOR BLUES FOR REV. GARY—PREPARATION

Our first fingerstyle piece has a right-hand pattern that is repeated in every measure. The thumb *(p)* alternates between two of the lower strings in each chord; this is called an *alternating bass*. When using alternating bass in the blues, the bass notes played with the thumb on beats 2 and 4 are often slightly accented: 1, **2,** 3, **4.**

Watch the right-hand fingering (indicated next to the notes in standard music notation) and the left-hand fingering (indicated under the TAB staff)—and keep it steady. The progression is a 16-bar minor blues that is based on the classic song, "Motherless Children." Like all blues standards, it was played by many performers. Rev. Gary Davis's rendition is probably the most popular. Our arrangement is not even close to the complexity of his, but it has the same chord progression. Many other songs are based on this progression. If we change each minor chord to a major or dominant 7, we get the chord progression for "When the Saints Go Marching In."

MINOR BLUES FOR REV. GARY

BLUES FOR MISSISSIPPI JOHN—PREPARATION

Learn to play pieces by Mississippi John Hurt. You'll love them. He played in the alternating bass style and sang up-tempo and fun songs. Also, his music is easier to play than the work of many other famous blues performers, so it's a good choice for a beginner.

This 12-bar blues on page 88 is typical of his pieces in G. Accent the second and fourth beats and watch the slide up to the 7th fret in bar 9.

In bars 5 and 6, you'll need to hold the notes of a C chord while stretching your 4th finger to fret the E♭. If this stretch is too difficult in the 1st *position* (position indicates where your 1st finger is located—in this case, the 1st fret), you can place a *capo* on the neck and play the piece in a higher position. A capo is a type of clamp that a guitarist can place on the neck to change the pitch of the music they are playing. Capos allow you to change keys without learning new fingerings. The frets get smaller as we move up the neck, so stretches are easier in higher positions. Practice your stretches by moving the capo lower as time goes on. As you play more and more, your fingers will become more agile, flexible and capable of longer stretches.

PHOTO · COURTESY OF VANGUARD

Mississippi John Hurt began playing guitar in 1903. A farm laborer, he developed his unique fingerpicking style in obscurity. It wasn't until the folk revival of the 1950s and 1960s that he received recognition by a mass audience. Suddenly, he found himself making more money than he ever thought possible. Until months before his death, he continued to record and perform as an artist who was in his prime.

BLUES FOR MISSISSIPPI JOHN

Track 81

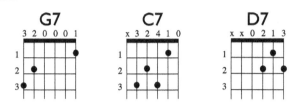

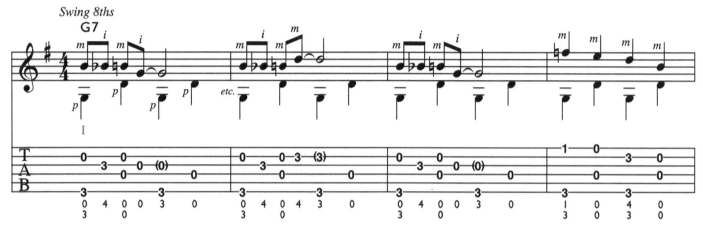

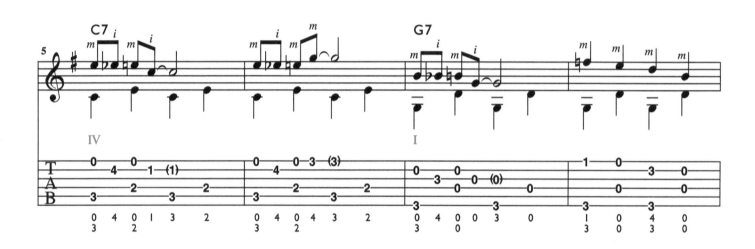

The early acoustic players like Robert Johnson, Blind Lemon Jefferson, Blind Blake and others played 12-bar progressions. They also played many songs based on other common patterns. The 16-bar chord sequence in "Keep On Pickin'" (page 90) is found in many songs including "Keep on Truckin'." This tune was played by many early players and was also recorded by Hot Tuna. Arlo Guthrie's "Alice's Restaurant" is also based on a similar progression. This style, which can be called *ragtime blues,* has a bouncy alternating bass—and it has more chords and quicker chord changes than 12-bar pieces.

For the C chords, the alternating bass starts with a C on the 5th string, moves to E on the 4th string, to G on the 6th string and back to E on the 4th string. To fret the G, just lift your 3rd finger off the C and place it on the 6th string, 3rd fret. We could finger the C chord with our 4th finger on the C and 3rd finger on the G and hold all the notes at the same time. If we move the 3rd finger from string to string, however, we will get a bass sound that is more characteristic of this type of piece.

Below are the chords you will need to play "Keep On Pickin'." The fingering for the F chord—with the left-hand thumb playing the root—is common, but if your thumb can't make the reach, use the barre fingering for the F instead.

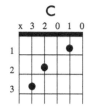

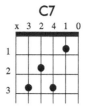

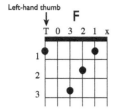

KEEP ON PICKIN'

Most fingerstyle blues pieces can be divided into two categories. In one category, pieces are based on the alternating bass. In the other, the thumb repeats a root-note on the lower strings. This style is sometimes called *Texas blues* and was used by the great Lightnin' Hopkins. Unlike ragtime blues, this style is not totally based on chords. Instead, a player will keep a steady beat on a low note and play melodic phrases or licks on the upper strings. There will be a few chords added here and there. This way of playing creates a full sound and is excellent for playing solo. When you get this going, you'll really sound like a blues player.

Texas blues is almost always played in the keys of E and A because in these keys, most of our important root notes are on open strings. This allows our left hand to play phrases on the upper strings in any position.

"Blues for Lightnin'" is based on the E Minor Pentatonic scale and contains a few popular blues licks. Notice that in measure 3, the E-note is played on the open 1st string and also on the 2nd string, 5th fret. Alternating between an open note and the unison fretted on the next string is a popular blues technique. Be careful with the slides, pull-offs and vibrato in this piece. It is a good idea to practice them separately.

Play the upper-string three-note E7, A7 and B7 chords by brushing upward lightly with your index finger. Be sure to keep your thumb steady on the repeated root-notes. No one will call the "blues police" if you miss a note, but it will not sound as good.

BLUES FOR LIGHTNIN'
Track 83

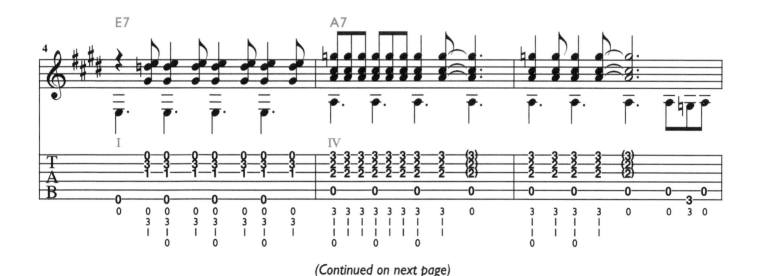

(Continued on next page)

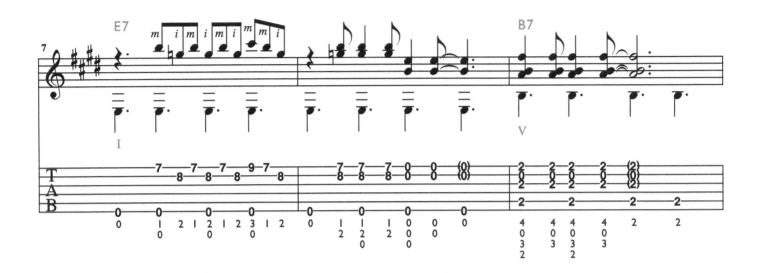

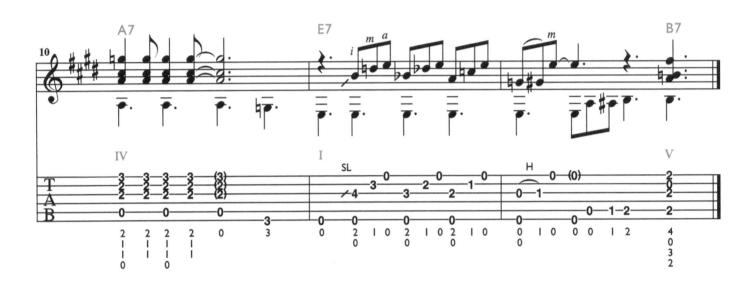

Jimmie Rodgers, who left the railroad and began his musical career in the 1920s, is nowadays called "The Father of Country Music." However, even a title that prestigious only begins to address the scope of his accomplishments. His influence has been felt not only in country music, but also in the folk and blues music that were a major part of his unique style.

BOOGIE WOOGIE TIME—PREPARATION

We covered boogie woogie style in Chapter 8 (page 43). Now we will play a boogie woogie pattern in which the thumb plays the lower strings while chords are played on the upper strings. It should almost sound like two people playing at the same time. Since the parts are so independent, you will probably find this piece more interesting than the others in this section. Boogie woogie pieces are usually played at fast tempos. As usual, have patience and keep at it. When you master this piece, you'll love to play it, and it will be an impressive addition to your repertoire.

Practice each section of the piece separately and keep the tempo very slow at first. Playing the phrases slowly will get them under your fingers. It will help you memorize them and allow them to "sink in." Throughout measures 1–6, you'll need to hold down the G$\sharp$ on the 3rd string while other fingers stretch to the 4th fret for certain bass notes. If at the moment this is too much of a stretch, use the capo and play the piece starting on a higher fret. Another option is to omit the G$\sharp$ and just play the open 1st and 2nd strings. This will not sound as good, but will be much easier. You can always add the G$\sharp$ later, when your stretching improves.

Unlike "Blues for Lightnin'," here we want to use our *i*, *m* and *a* fingers to pluck the upper strings for a cleaner sound.

*To many, the music of **Robert Johnson** is the epitome of the blues. In 1930, partly inspired by bluesman Son House, Johnson left the world of sharecropping to become a full-time musician. In his short career, he recorded 29 songs. These intense recordings represent some of the most influential blues music ever produced.*

BOOGIE WOOGIE TIME

APPENDIX

Chord Fingerings

The chords on this page—along with the barre chord fingerings in Chapter 16 (page 79)—will get you through most blues situations.

Dominant 7 Fingerings—Open or 1st position

A7	A7	B7	C7	D7
	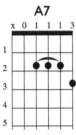	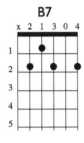	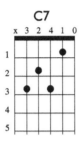	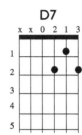

E7	E7	F7	G7
		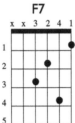	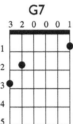

Major and Minor Fingerings—Open or 1st position

These are not as common in the blues as dominant 7s, but are still important to master.

A	C	D	E	F
	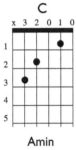	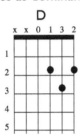		

G	Amin	Bmin	Dmin	Emin
	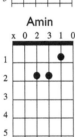		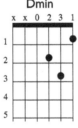	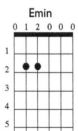

Closed Voicings

These shapes are moveable. Slide them up or down the neck until you reach the root-note you need. The second dominant 7 shape has the same fingering as the C7 in open position, but here we need to mute the 1st string so we can play the chord on any fret. Be sure to mute the open strings in each of these voicings.

7	7	9	min7	Maj7
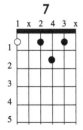	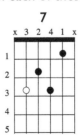	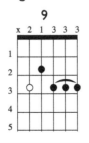		

FINAL THOUGHTS

Congratulations on completing the first section of this book!

Hopefully, you are having a great time playing the acoustic blues. Now here is some advice to help you grow as a musician.

Play often, regularly and with passion. Learn everything between these covers. Every chapter is filled with techniques that all blues players need to know.

It may take awhile, but try to memorize everything in this book. Memorize the notes in every common scale and chord. This will increase your confidence and make the music a part of you.

Write out and practice each example in all the common keys. This will familiarize you with the fretboard and will prepare you for new musical situations. You'll be ready for anything.

Playing along with albums will improve your musical ear. Figure out the key and the chords and play along with the band. If you can't figure out what the guitarist on the recording is doing, make up your own part. Improvise along with the recording. Also, try to figure out parts of the solos. If you can't get the exact notes, try to imitate the rhythms. This gets easier the more you do it.

Writing your own music is a real thrill. Take standard progressions and add new melodies and lyrics; or add new twists to tried-and-true patterns. Borrow ideas, but always try to add something new and original.

Learn to play with others. As soon as you can play a blues progression, stick your guitar neck out and say "let's jam." Music is a team sport. You'll learn faster and have a great time. Other players have been where you are, so they'll probably be patient with you. Play at open mics, parties, nursing homes, etc. Share your music. Applause is hard to beat—addictive, yet healthy for your soul.

Keep learning any way you can. A good teacher will help, as will other books and videos. Rob Fletcher's *Blues Grooves for Guitar* (Alfred Music #21895) will give you a complete look at blues rhythm guitar. Also, if you're interested in fingerstyle or country blues, check out my book *Beginning Fingerstyle Guitar* (Alfred Music #14099).

The blues is a vocal music, so start singing. Most blues tunes are based on progressions in this book. Get the lyrics, open your mouth and let the music come out. You don't have to be Pavarotti to sing the blues. You just have to be yourself. So be yourself, play the blues and have fun.

If you have questions or comments about this book, you can write to loumanzi@snet.net.

INTERMEDIATE
ACOUSTIC

BLUES GUITAR

Audio tracks recorded by Jason Alborough at WorkshopLive.com, Pittsfield, MA

TABLE OF CONTENTS

ABOUT THIS BOOK

Welcome to the *Intermediate* section of *The Complete Acoustic Blues Guitar Method*. In this section, you will find many exciting techniques and concepts used by leading players of today and yesterday. Though it is intended for acoustic players, it also features material common to both the acoustic and electric guitar. The material in this section is designed for someone who already knows the basic blues "moves" and wants their playing to sound more interesting or professional.

This section introduces many new concepts and techniques, while taking those covered in the previous section to exciting new levels. You'll learn new chords and scales, improve your blues soloing and learn some cool new fingerstyle pieces.

Enjoy!

00

Track 1

Online audio is included with this book to make learning easier and more enjoyable. The symbol shown on the left appears next to every example in the book that features an audio track. Use the recordings to ensure you're capturing the feel of the examples and interpreting the rhythms correctly. The track number below the symbol corresponds directly to the example you want to hear (example numbers are above the icon). All the track numbers are unique to each "book" within this volume, meaning every book has its own Track 1, Track 2, and so on. (For example, *Beginning Acoustic Blues Guitar* starts with Track 1, as does *Intermediate Acoustic Blues Guitar* and *Mastering Acoustic Blues Guitar*.) Track 1 for each book will help you tune your guitar.

See page 1 for instructions on how to access the online audio.

CHAPTER 1
Blues Rhythm

RHYTHMIC NOTATION

Rhythm refers to patterns of long and short sounds and silences. *Rhythmic notation* is used to show these patterns when playing chords.

Rhythmic Notation Values

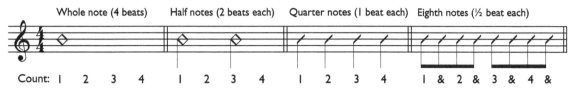

Sometimes just the chord name is written above the staff. Sometimes a *chord diagram* (see illustration to the right) is placed above the staff.

or
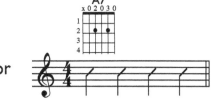

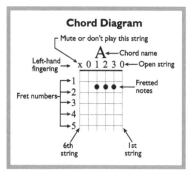

BASIC STRUMS

Let's start with a couple basic rhythms before moving on to more involved blues strums. Count a steady "1, 2, 3, 4" and tap your foot on each beat. Now strum an E7 chord (see diagram to the right) in quarter notes—one strum per beat. This symbol ⊓ indicates a *downstroke* (strum or pick downward). Notice the sharps at the beginning of the staff. This is the *key signature*, which tells you all the notes that are either sharp or flat throughout the entire piece. This example is in the key of E.

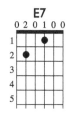

⊓ = Downstroke

Track 2

Now let's strum steady eighth notes—two strums per beat. Be sure to count the rhythm as indicated under the staff (1–&, 2–&, etc.). This symbol V indicates an *upstroke* (strum or pick upward).

V = Upstroke

Track 3

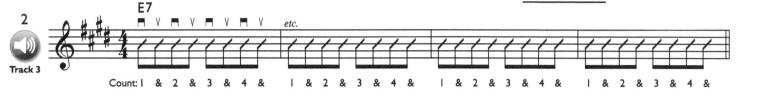

Musicians talk about rhythmic "feel." This is the characteristic rhythm or pulse of a tune. Using this hip musical term, we would say that most blues has a *triplet feel*. The rest of this chapter explains what the triplet feel is all about. Listening to the recording that comes with this book will help you to understand and play the following rhythms.

TRIPLETS

A *triplet* is three notes played in the time of two notes of the same value. It is indicated by a "3" placed above or below the group of notes. An *eighth-note triplet* divides a beat evenly between three eighth notes.

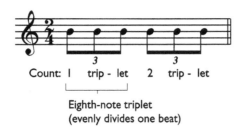

Now we'll strum triplets. Keep it steady and count as indicated under the staff. Tap your foot down on the *onbeats* (the first part of each beat indicated by numbers).

%. = Repeat previous measure

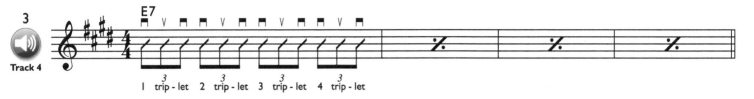

We can also play the first and last notes of a triplet, giving the first note the value of a quarter note. Count "1–trip-let, 2–trip-let," etc., but just strum on the onbeats and "let."

Now let's combine both of our triplet figures in the next example.

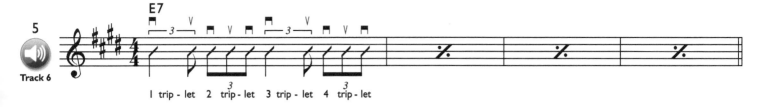

$\frac{12}{8}$ RHYTHM

The rhythm from example 5 (page 102) can also be written in $\frac{12}{8}$ time. In this time signature there are 12 beats in a bar, with each eighth note getting one beat. You can think of it, however, as having four beats in each measure and count it as indicated in the example below. This maintains the triplet feel.

Track 6
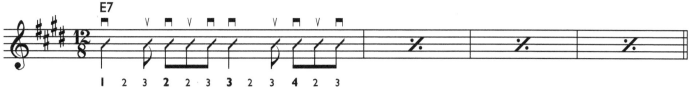

SWING EIGHTHS

In the blues, eighth notes are not usually played exactly as notated. Rather, they are interpreted in a *swing* or *shuffle* style. *Swing eighth* notes look exactly like "straight" eighth notes, but are played like the first and last notes of a triplet.

In this book, this swing rhythm is indicated with the caption: *Swing 8ths.*

This next example uses swing eighths and sounds exactly the same as the previous two examples (5 and 6).

Track 6

Our next example starts with a *pickup*. This is a note or group of notes before the first full measure. Count a full measure of four beats, then come in on the "&" of beat 3. Theoretically, the missing beats of the pickup measure are borrowed from the last measure, which is also incomplete. Also, note that the numbers under the TAB staff indicate left-hand finger numbers.

Track 7
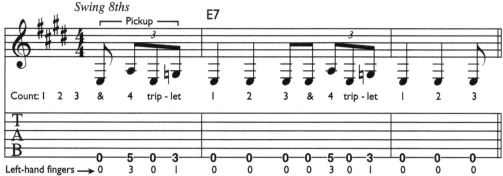

CHAPTER 2

Blues Theory

A *phrase* is a musical statement or idea. What makes a blues phrase sound so distinctive and evocative? We may not be able to explain all the emotions behind the notes in a blues piece or solo, but we can discuss the musical resources players use to express those emotions.

A good understanding of basic major scale theory (page 35) is essential at this point. We will be defining characteristic blues sounds by relating them to the degrees of the major scale (1–2–3–4–5–6–7–8). We can alter any of these tones by placing an accidental in front of them (for example: ♭2). This changes the distance between the 1 and the degree that is altered. For instance, from a 1 to a 2 is a whole step. A flat (♭) lowers a note a half step. So the distance from a 1 to a ♭2 is a half step.

THE ♭3, ♭7 AND ♭5

There are three colorful sounds—known as *blue notes*—that are essential to the blues style: the ♭3, ♭7 and ♭5. A phrase doesn't need to have all three of these to sound like the blues, but it would be difficult to get that sound without at least one of them.

Since E is perhaps the most popular blues guitar key (see page 41, Diatonic Harmony), we'll use it for the examples in this section. Here is an E Major scale. Notice that the 3rd note is G♯, the 5th note is B and the 7th is D♯.

E Major Scale

THE ♭3

In the key of E, a ♭3 is a G♮. The short phrase below demonstrates how a blues sound can be achieved with only a tonic (1) and this cool flat-3rd (♭3) sound. Notice in the following examples that the chord names are gray. This indicates the general harmony or chord sound that goes with the phrase. Have a friend strum the chords while you play the *licks* (phrases).

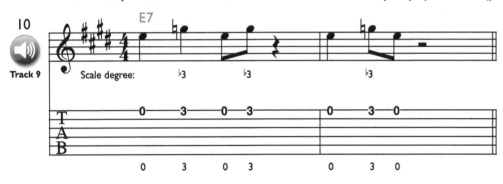

THE ♭3/♮3 COMBINATION

Notice in the chord diagram to the right, an E7 includes a G♯ (♮3), which clashes with the G♮ (♭3). This clash creates *dissonance* or a "harsh" sound. In some musical styles, this would be considered a mistake, but in the blues it's *essential*. Players often use the ♭3 and the ♮3 in the same phrase.

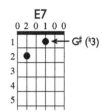

This next example adds these notes to the first and second notes of the major scale (E and F♯). Note that the ♭3 will often resolve to the ♮3.

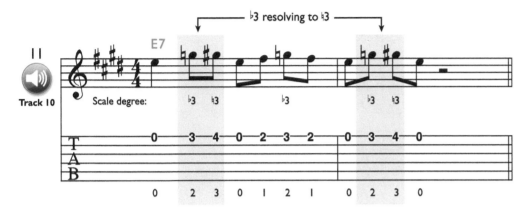

THE ♭7

It's really unusual to find a ♮7 in a blues piece. The ♭7 is our standard 7th sound. In the key of E, the ♭7 is a D♮. This note appears in several scales we'll look at later in this book. Try this next example.

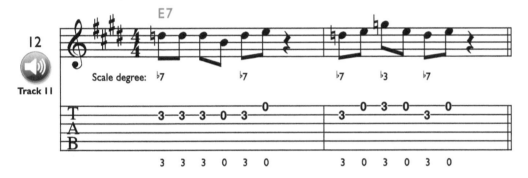

THE ♭5

The ♭5 is not used quite as often as the ♭3 and ♭7, but it is a colorful and crucial blues sound. In the key of E, the ♭5 is B♭. This note usually resolves up to the ♮5 or down to the 4.

The following example contains all three of our blue notes.

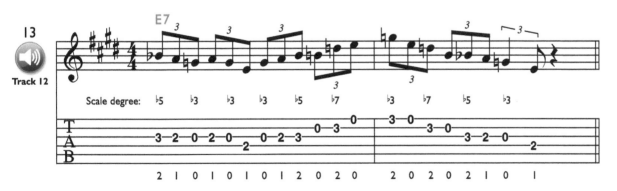

Throughout this book, you'll be advised to change examples and pieces to other keys. This is called *transposing*. It's easy to transpose if you know your diatonic harmony. To help you better understand, we'll need to refer to the chart below, which illustrates the diatonic harmony of each major key.

I	ii	iii	IV	V	vi	vii°	I
C	Dmin	Emin	F	G	Amin	Bdim	C
G	Amin	Bmin	C	D	Emin	F#dim	G
D	Emin	F#min	G	A	Bmin	C#dim	D
A	Bmin	C#min	D	E	F#min	G#dim	A
E	F#min	G#min	A	B	C#min	D#dim	E
B	C#min	D#min	E	F#	G#min	A#dim	B
F#	G#min	A#min	B	C#	D#min	E#dim	F#
G♭	A♭min	B♭min	C♭	D♭	E♭min	Fdim	G♭
D♭	E♭min	Fmin	G♭	A♭	B♭min	Cdim	D♭
A♭	B♭min	Cmin	D♭	E♭	Fmin	Gdim	A♭
E♭	Fmin	Gmin	A♭	B♭	Cmin	Ddim	E♭
B♭	Cmin	Dmin	E♭	F	Gmin	Adim	B♭
F	Gmin	Amin	B♭	C	Dmin	Edim	F

Let's say you're playing a simple *chord progression,* or series of chords, in the key of A. A is the I chord, D is the IV and E is the V.

Slash notation. Play any form of the chord you like (unless indicated in a chord diagram above) in the rhythm you choose.

Now you want to transpose it to the key of C. Take a look at the diatonic harmony chart above and find the row for the key of C. You'll notice that C is the I, F is the IV and G is V. If your piece started with one bar of A, now you'll play one bar of C. If you then had a bar of D, you'll play one bar of F. The next two bars—instead of A and E—would now be C and G.

What you are doing is following the same Roman-numeral chord pattern, but replacing the original chords with the corresponding chords from your new key. You can also use the chart to transpose phrases and *riffs* (short repeated melodic patterns). Just play single notes rather than chords. Eventually, you will be able to transpose into common keys from memory.

CHAPTER 3

Blues Progressions

The standard musical *form* (structure) used in the blues is the *12-bar blues progression*. It is 12 bars long and is almost always in $\frac{4}{4}$ time. In essence, although there are many variations, it consists of three chords that progress in standard patterns.

In the *Beginning* section, the most popular 12-bar blues progressions were introduced. We'll review these quickly in this chapter, but with some twists and variations. We'll also learn some new progressions.

We can identify a blues progression by its Roman numerals. For example, a I–IV progression would be C to F in the key of C, but would be G to C in the key of G.

	I →IV
Key of C:	C → F
Key of G:	G → C

The particular chords will change when you change keys, but the progression will still be identified as a I–IV progression. This makes it easy for musicians to communicate chord progressions. For example, you might hear, "It's a iii–vi–ii–V–I progression in the key of B♭." What they're referring to is the following chord progression: Dmin(iii)–Gmin(vi)–Cmin(ii)–F(V)–B♭(I).

Take a look at the diatonic harmony chart on the previous page and memorize the I, IV and V chords in the popular blues keys. These are A, B, C, D, E, F, G and B♭. Then you need to know the Roman-numeral pattern for each of our standard progressions and learn to play them from memory in these keys.

EASIEST 12-BAR BLUES

In *Beginning Acoustic Blues Guitar,* we learned the "Easiest 12-Bar Blues," which has fewer chord changes than other common blues progressions and consists of:

- Four bars of I
- Two bars of IV
- Two bars of I
- Two bars of V
- Two bars of I

Note that these Roman numerals correspond to the root notes of the chords. It is standard in the blues to go outside of diatonic harmony (page 41) and make all the chords dominant 7th chords. This is an essential sound of the blues.

The B♭ version on page 108 combines four-note chord voicings with a cool riff at the end of each bar. Watch the eighth rests; the strums should be short and choppy. Once you've got it rolling in B♭, transpose (see page 106) it to other keys. This is easy, because the chords and riffs are *movable,* which means, because they have no open strings, you can move them to different places on the neck without affecting the musical relationships within them. Just move the fingerings to correspond to new root notes. For example, if you were to play the piece in the key of A, you would just move everything down one fret. The tune would sound the same, only a little bit lower. You should try transposing most of the material in this book to various keys. Not only will it help you better understand your instrument and music in general, but it will also prepare you for a variety of musical situations.

The chords for "12-Bar Blues in B♭" are *movable* chords. This means you can move the shapes anywhere on the neck and maintain the same qualities. For example, if you move the B♭7 chord down a fret, you get an A7 chord. Notice there are hollow dots ○ in the chord diagrams. These indicate the roots of chords and are included in the diagrams of all movable chords.

12-BAR BLUES IN B♭

Track 13

This next piece—in the key of E—uses one of the most popular progressions in the blues. The "Most Common 12-Bar Blues" consists of:

- One bar of I
- One bar of IV
- Two bars of I
- Two bars of IV
- Two bars of I
- One bar of V
- One bar of IV
- One bar of I
- One bar of V

The rhythm of "Quick-Four Blues" involves chords that anticipate the next measure; instead of playing the chord on beat 1, it is played on the final *offbeat* (the second half of each beat represented by "&") of the previous measure. This occurs in bars 1, 3, 5, 7, 9 and 11. Rhythms like this are called *syncopated,* which means the emphasis is shifted from the onbeats to the offbeats. This gives the music lots of drive and forward momentum. The move to a IV chord in the second bar is called a *quick four.*

QUICK-FOUR BLUES

Track 14

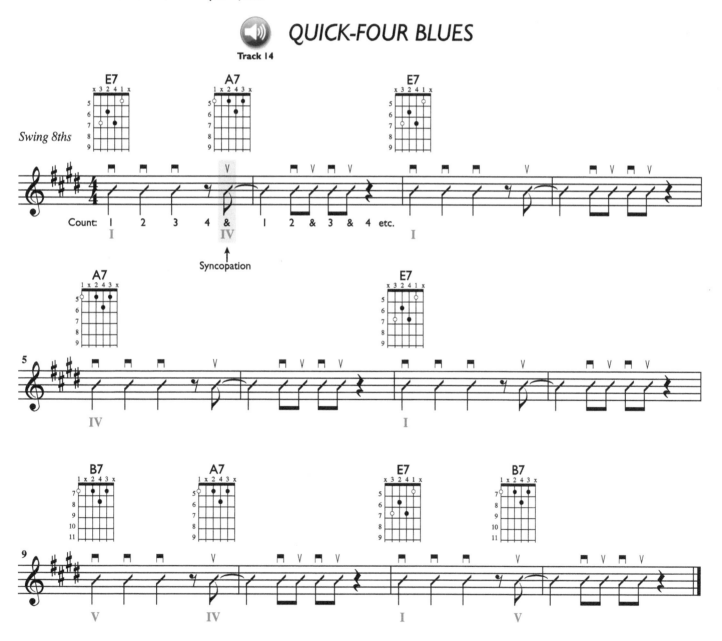

This next piece follows the "Easiest 12-Bar Blues" until the last measure, where it follows the "Most Common 12-Bar Blues" by going to a V chord. "Mojo Blues" has a rhythmic style similar to Muddy Waters's recording of "Got My Mojo Working." We have a straight eighth rhythm, where all the chords are played with downstrokes. The dot over every other strum indicates *staccato*. This tells us to play the strum short and choppy. To achieve this, quickly release left-hand pressure after each staccato strum. This simple, yet exciting piece should really get your Mojo working!

MOJO BLUES

Track 15

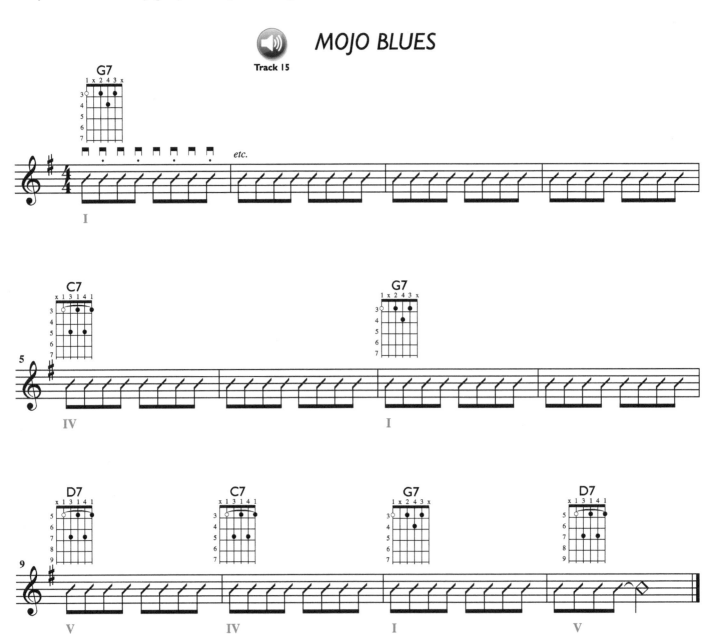

The *16-bar blues* is a 16-measure blues form that progresses in standard patterns. Our next tune is based on the most common 16-bar blues form and is in the style of Muddy Waters' "Hoochie Coochie Man." Think of it as a 12-bar blues with four extra bars of the I chord at the beginning. This form is a nice change from the standard 12-bar forms and is great to play at gigs where you're getting paid by the measure. Watch the pickup notes in the first measure. Also, in the last measure, there is a *slide* (SL), which is accomplished by picking a fretted note and—maintaining finger pressure on the string—sliding to a second note on the same string. Slides can be played ascending or descending. The slide in the last measure is an *unspecified slide,* for which a starting location is not given. With this type of slide, you would usually start from one to three frets below the destination note.

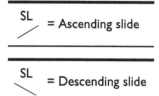

SL ╱ = Ascending slide

SL ╲ = Descending slide

𝅘𝅥 = *Staccato.* Play sharp, pointed.

HOOCHIE BLUES

Track 16

The *9-bar blues?* Is that legal? The answer is *yes*, and here's one for you to play. Though not as popular as the other forms, the 9-bar blues can create variety in a set of tunes. This tune is in the style of Howlin' Wolf's recording of "Sittin' On Top of the World." The D♭7 chord in bar 4 is considered a *flat-six* (♭VI). The diatonic vi chord in the key of F would be a Dmin. In standard blues fashion, we turned it into a dominant 7th chord. Then we flatted the whole chord, producing a D♭7—another cool blues move. Also, bar 8 features another great left-hand technique—the *hammer-on*. To play a hammer-on, pick one note and sound the next note on the same string by "hammering-on" with a left-hand finger. The second note is not picked. To do this effectively, you need to bring your left-hand finger down cleanly on the fret, just behind the fret wire. Think of tapping the note with your left-hand finger, rather than just fretting it. In a good hammer-on, each note will be equal in volume. A curved line ⌢ called a slur, connecting one note to a higher note, indicates a hammer-on. The first notes of the hammer-ons in the tune below are *grace notes*. A grace note is an *ornament*, meant to *decorate* the melody. It is not given a value of its own but proceeds quickly to the destination note. Also, be sure to memorize the turnaround and use it in other pieces as well.

⌢H = Hammer-on

WOLF'S BLUES

Track 17

A *dot* adds half the value of a note to itself. In ¹²⁄₈ time, a quarter note gets 2 beats. Half the value of 2 is 1. 2 + 1 = 3. A *dotted quarter note* in ¹²⁄₈ time gets 3 beats.

CHAPTER 4

Shuffles and Two-String Patterns

Go to any blues show and chances are you're going to hear two things:

1. Someone will probably sing "I got up this morning" (even if they didn't wake up until the afternoon).

2. Lots of *two-string shuffle* patterns.

We learned some basic two-string shuffle patterns in *Beginning Acoustic Blues Guitar*. These are played in swing eighths rhythm and are based on *double stops* (two notes played at the same time) made of a root and a 5. To be a good blues player, you need to provide lots of variations in this style. The more you know, the more interesting and exciting your playing will be.

In this chapter, we'll add more colorful licks and rhythms to the material covered in the first book. You should memorize these pieces and transpose them to other keys as well. You'll have fun with these examples and can use them at a gig, or even when you're just sitting around the house jamming with friends.

PALM MUTING

You'll need to *palm mute* (P.M.) some of the music in this chapter. This important technique was also covered in detail in the first book of this series. If you are new to palm muting, it will be easy to incorporate it into your playing. Just rest the fleshy part of your palm—down where your palm meets your wrist and heads toward the pinky—on the exact spot where the strings touch the bridge of your guitar. Don't press down too hard—just let your palm rest lightly. This will give you a muted, percussive tone that is an essential blues sound. Try to imitate the sound on the recording that comes with this book. Listen to this example.

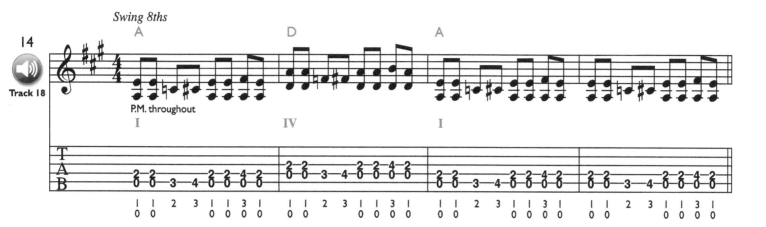

Notice that the 6 is part of the pattern on which "Shuffle in A" is based. Also, as we saw on page 105, the move from the ♭3 to the ♮3 is a characteristic sound of the blues. This classic move is featured on the second beat of almost every measure. Be sure to palm mute the strings when you play "Shuffle in A."

SHUFFLE IN A

Track 19

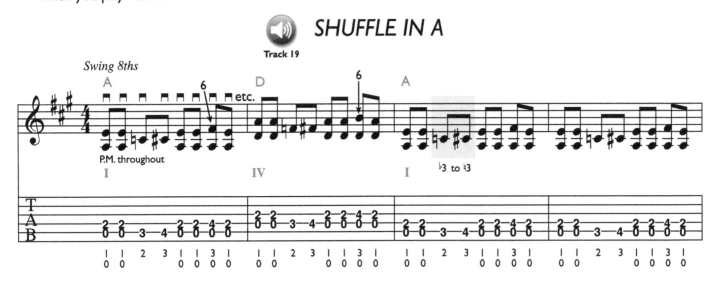

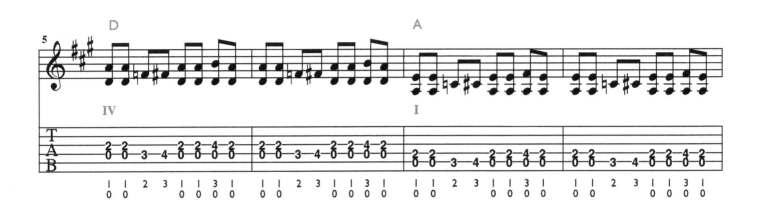

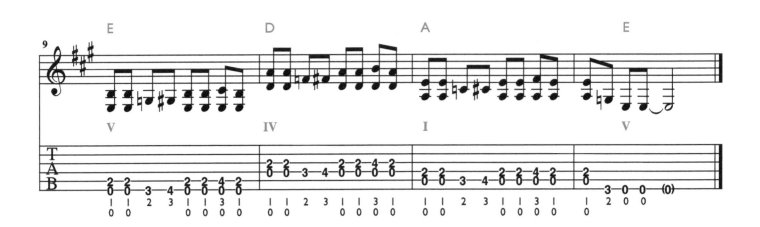

This piece also features the ♭3/♮3 move. It's similar to "Shuffle in A" (page 114), but differs in that it's in the key of E and has a straight eighth rhythm. Once again, add palm muting to the mix.

STRAIGHT 8THS IN E

Track 20

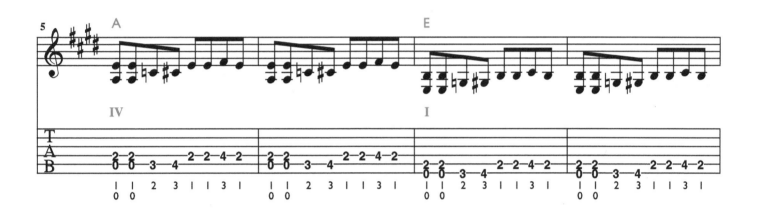

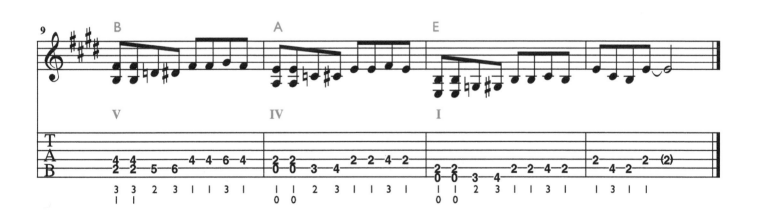

The ♭7 produces another important sound in the blues. It appears on the second beat of most bars in this next piece. Check out the cool descending lower string line at the end. It's worth transposing phrases like this to other keys and adding them to your bag of blues tricks.

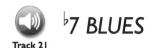

♭7 BLUES

Track 21

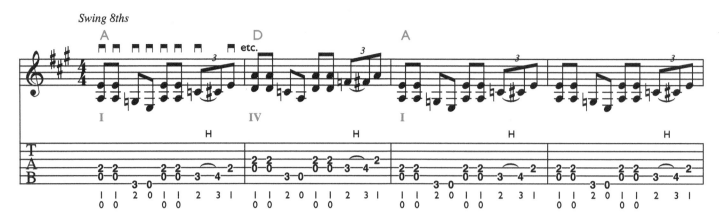

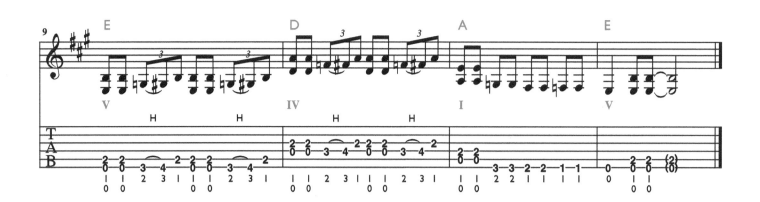

The top line in our next piece goes from a 5 to a 6 to a ♭7. It then skips down to the ♭3 before moving on to a ♮3 and the rest of the measure. This gives it a strong and colorful sound. You'll hear pieces like this in the work of Muddy Waters and other blues masters.

BLUES FOR MUDDY

Track 22

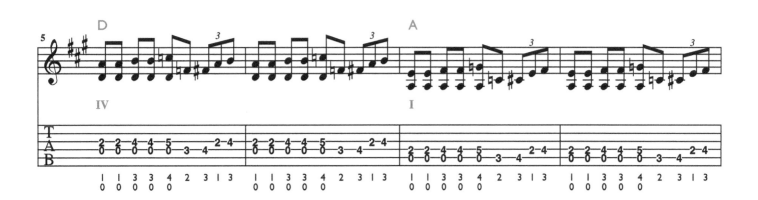

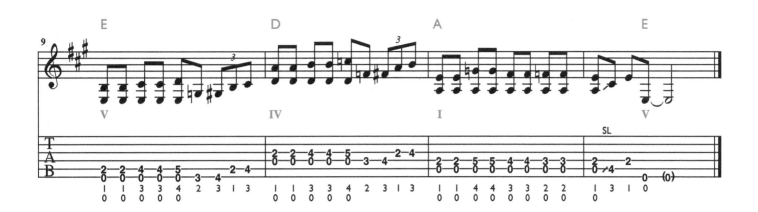

As we've seen with the tunes in this chapter so far, the keys of A and E lend themselves to double-note patterns that include open strings. It's important, however, to learn these patterns in forms that are movable and have no open strings. This way you can play them anywhere on the neck and in any key. This piece in C uses movable two-string patterns, starts with a pickup and has a syncopated rhythm.

SYNCOPATED BLUES IN C

Track 23

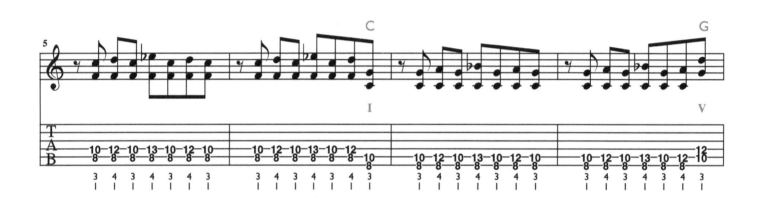

In $\frac{4}{4}$ time, a dotted quarter note gets one-and-a-half beats ($1 + \frac{1}{2} = 1\frac{1}{2}$)

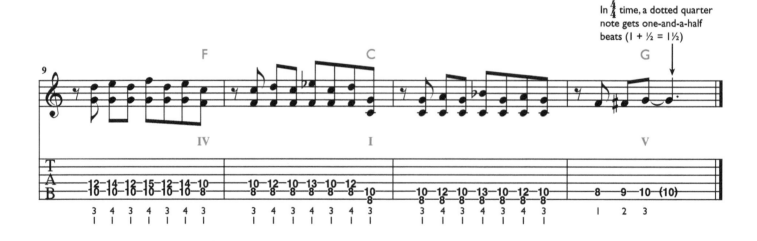

CHAPTER 5

Soloing

We've all heard the masters play solos expressing the range of human emotion—from the heights of joy to the depths of sorrow. As a soloist, it's important to find the "soul" within you and put it into your music. The scales for *improvisation* (spontaneous musical composition) are just *tools* for our expression.

The three types of scales covered in this chapter are the most important for a blues player to know. Practice them all until you have them memorized and are comfortable with them. Make sure each note rings clearly and gradually increase your speed. Learn to play them in all the natural keys and work on creating your own solos and phrases.

LEFT-HAND TECHNIQUE REVIEW

The musical examples in this chapter include a variety of left-hand techniques. We've already looked at hammer-ons (page 112) and slides (page 111). We'll also be using *pull-offs, bends* and *vibrato.*

PULL-OFF

A pull-off is accomplished by picking a fretted note, then "pulling-off" with the left-hand finger that is fretting the note. This activates a lower note on the same string.

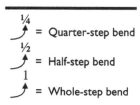

BEND

A bend—one of the most expressive techniques in the blues—is often used to imitate the phrasing of the human voice. A bend is accomplished by playing a fretted note and bending—or pushing—the string to arrive at the pitch of another note. When bending, we need to have a destination note in mind. In acoustic blues, we use *quarter-step* (half of a half step), *half-step* and *whole-step bends.* In TAB and standard music notation, bends are indicated by a curved arrow. The number above the arrow tells us if it is a quarter-, half- or whole-step bend.

VIBRATO

Vibrato is a series of quick, tiny bends and is often used on the final note of a phrase, or any other sustained note. To use this technique, play a fretted note anywhere on the neck. Pretend to "itch" the note after you pick it, by moving your finger slightly up and down. Be sure to keep pressure on the note and you will hear the pitch fluctuate. Try to keep this fluctuation even. Vibrato can be fast or slow depending upon the speed of your movement. It can also be wide or narrow depending on how far the finger moves from its starting spot. Vibrato is indicated by a wavy line.

The *minor pentatonic scale* consists of scale degrees: 1–♭3–4–5–♭7. In the key of A, our notes are: A–C–D–E–G. Below is the three-octave A Minor Pentatonic scale in standard music notation and TAB.

A Minor Pentatonic Scale

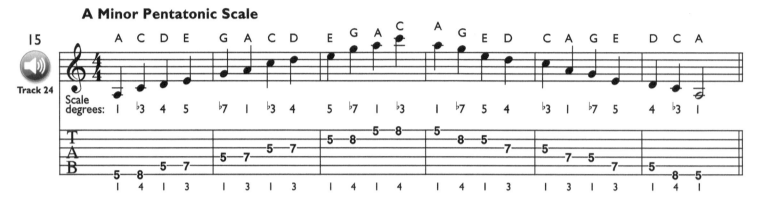

Here it is in diagram form. Scale degrees are indicated inside the dots. The hollow dots indicate the tonic notes of the scale.

A Minor Pentatonic Scale

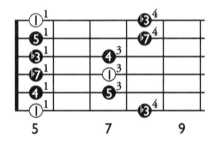

The *lick* (short, musical phrase) below is based on the A Minor Pentatonic scale and includes vibrato, bends and slides. Start your slides from three frets below your destination note. In the bend, the C (♭3) goes up a quarter step in pitch to the sound *between* C and C♯ (the ♮3) and never really reaches the C♯. This is a common blues move. We say that the "blues" sounds are really *between* the notes. Let's try it.

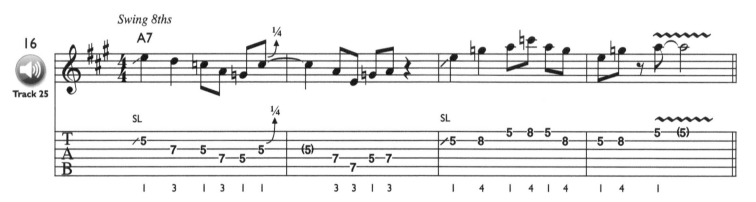

Our next example is based on the B Minor Pentatonic scale. Here, we are adding double stops to the mix. The first double stop is a *tritone* (the distance between a 1 and a ♭5) that includes a G♯. This note does not belong to the minor pentatonic scale, but produces a cool dissonance when coupled with the D.

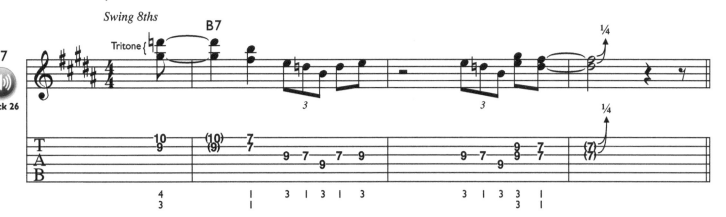

MINOR PENTATONIC SCALE WITH EXTENSION

Below is another fingering for the A Minor Pentatonic scale. It is the same as the previous fingering, but shifts to a higher position when you get to the 3rd string. This extends the range of notes we can use.

A Minor Pentatonic Scale (with Extension)

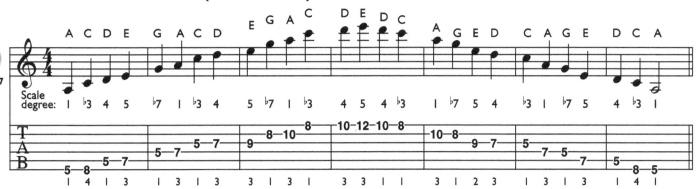

A Minor Pentatonic Scale (with Extension)

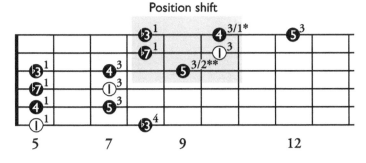

* 3rd finger ascending/1st finger descending
** 3rd finger ascending/2nd finger descending

The hammer-ons that start the next example need to be hit really fast. We don't want the grace notes to stand out—just add impact to the destination note. This example is based on a G Minor Pentatonic scale and makes use of the upper notes of the minor pentatonic scale extension.

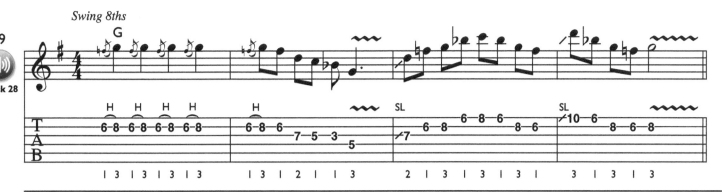

MAJOR PENTATONIC SCALE

The *major pentatonic scale* consists of scale degrees: 1–2–3–5–6. In the key of A, these notes are: A–B–C#–E–F#. It has a brighter sound than the minor pentatonic scale and does not have any flatted or altered scale degrees. Let's play it.

A Major Pentatonic Scale

A Major Pentatonic Scale

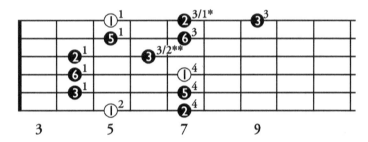

* 3rd finger ascending/1st finger descending
** 3rd finger ascending/2nd finger descending

Now, let's use this fingering in the key of D. The 1 or tonic would be on the 10th fret of the 6th string.

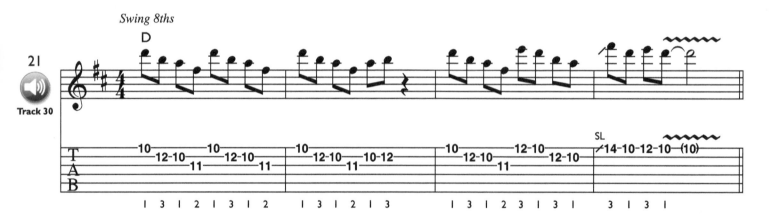

Here's an example in the key of C, so the tonic is on the 8th fret of the 6th string. For the pull-offs, you'll need to have your 1st finger already fretted before you start to pull-off with your 3rd finger. Also, for the triplet at the beginning of the third measure, lay your 1st finger across the top two strings at the 8th fret. This technique is called *barring* and will allow the hammered note on the 2nd string to ring and blend with the following note on the 1st string.

BLUES SCALE

Add a ♭5 to the minor pentatonic scale and you have the *blues scale*. It consists of scale degrees: 1–♭3–4–♭5–♮5–♭7. In the key of A, the notes are: A–C–D–E♭–E♮–G. It has a similar feel to the minor pentatonic scale, but the ♭5 gives the blues scale a funky edge and adds a lot of color. It's perhaps the "bluest" of the scales we use, with three blue notes—♭3, ♭5 and ♭7.

A Blues Scale

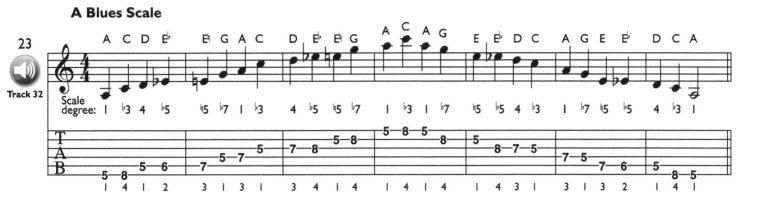

A Blues Scale

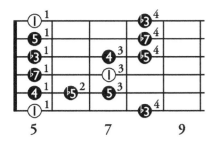

For a cool, edgy beginning to a phrase, try leading off with a ♭5.

This next example is based on the B Blues scale (the tonic is on the 7th fret of the 6th string). Hammering-on from the ♭5 to the ♮5 is a popular blues lick. Check it out in the example below. Note that, in the key of B, the ♭5 is an F♮ and the ♮5 is an F♯. Also, the slide in the 2nd full bar is a *measured slide*. This type of slide has a definite starting note, and both notes have their own rhythmic value (in this case, an eighth note sliding to a quarter note). The two notes are connected by a diagonal line and a slur ⌢.

Measured Slide

PHOTO COURTESY INSTITUTE OF JAZZ STUDIES, RUTGERS UNIVERSITY

*The sound of **Lightnin' Hopkins** (1912–1982) is the sound of Texas blues. He combined fast and furious licks on the upper strings with a thumping bass to create an exciting and influential style.*

So far, we've looked at each scale individually. This is a good way to familiarize yourself with each of them. However, it's common in the blues to use more than one scale in a solo (or even a phrase). These combinations of scales and notes create a colorful blend of sound. The example on page 126 ("Three Scales in 12 Bars") illustrates popular approaches to combining scales. The following bar-by-bar explanation of the phrases will give you ideas for your own solos and improvisations.

Bar 1, A7—The major pentatonic scale is often played over the I chord, as it is here. The ♮3 in the scale (C♯) matches the ♮3 in the A7 chord. The opening hammer-on from the ♭3 (C) to the ♮3 (C♯) is a classic blues move.

Bar 2, D7—The A Minor Pentatonic scale is used over the IV chord (D7). The ♭3 of the scale (C) matches the ♭7 of the D7 chord. This idea of using the I major pentatonic scale over the I chord and then the I minor pentatonic scale over the IV chord is a signature sound of combining scales in the blues.

Bars 3 and 4, A7—Here we start with the major pentatonic scale—throwing in a ♭7 (G) from the minor pentatonic scale—and move *chromatically* (in half steps) from E to C♯, with a final skip to the tonic (A).

Bar 5, D7—Here we go back to the minor pentatonic scale for a double-stop lick over the IV chord. Notice, however, there is an F♯ from the major pentatonic scale.

Bar 6, D7—The E♭ (♭5) that we've added turns the minor pentatonic scale into the blues scale.

Bar 7, A7—The major pentatonic scale is a popular choice for the I chord, but of course, it's not the only choice. Over this A7 we move to a higher position of the minor pentatonic scale. We're using *imitation* to tie the solo together; the last four notes in this bar are the same notes that started bar two—only an octave higher.

Bar 8, A7—The bend from D to E♭ (4 to ♭5) turns the minor pentatonic scale back into the blues scale.

Bar 9, E7—E7 is our V chord. Any one of our scales will work for this chord. In this example, we are using the A Minor Pentatonic scale.

Bar 10, D7—Here we have an example of *call and response*. This is when a musical statement, or call, is made, and then a musical response is given. Bar 9 is the call and bar 10 is the response. Notice the phrase is the same except for the ending. In call and response, we often repeat a phrase with a slight change.

Bar 11, A7—Here we go back to the I chord, and so back to the major pentatonic scale. For a little color, we throw in a ♭7 (G) from the minor pentatonic scale. Notice that this phrase is almost exactly the same as bar 3; imitation strikes again.

Bar 12, E7—Over this V chord, we have minor pentatonic scale notes ending on E, the 5th of the scale. The solo is over, so all we have to do is smile as we listen to our fans applaud.

THREE SCALES IN 12 BARS

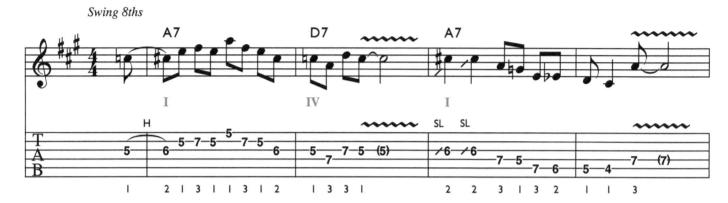

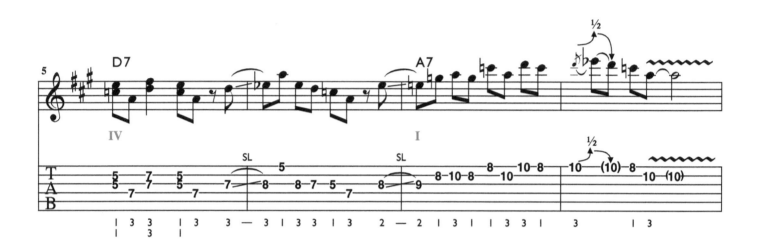

CHAPTER 6

Chord Voicings

Question: How do you play an E7 chord?
Answer: Many, many, many different ways.

On the guitar, any particular chord can be fingered in a variety of ways. This is one of the unique and challenging aspects of the guitar and because of it, we have an amazing array of chord sounds at our disposal. This can help make our music more interesting—both to us and our listeners.

We learned on page 38 that a *voicing* is a particular arrangement of notes in a chord. We'll assume you already know all of the open position fingerings for our most common blues chords. If you don't, you should get them under your belt (by going through the first book in this series) before you tackle these new shapes.

A chord is in *root position* when its root is the lowest note in the fingering. When any other chord tone is the lowest note, it's an *inversion*. Different inversions of a chord can be called different *voicings*.

TRIAD VOICINGS

As we learned on page 37, triads are three-note chords. In this section, we'll look at fingerings for major and minor triads on the top three strings. Once you learn the G Major and A Minor shapes, play them in different places on the neck. Remember, they take their names from their root notes. For example, if you move all the G Major triads up one whole step, they become A Major triads. Note that *root 1* tells you the root of the chord is on the 1st string; *root 2* means the root is on the 2nd string; etc. Scale degrees (chord tones) are at the bottom of each diagram.

G Major Voicings

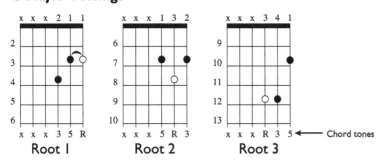

A Minor Voicings

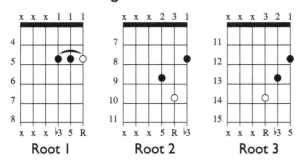

Below is a *minor blues* in A. Minor blues follow the standard blues forms, but consist mostly of minor chords. There is a sliding figure using the root-1 minor triad. Begin the slide from two frets below and press tightly to sustain the sound as you move up the frets.

SLIDING MINOR

Track 36

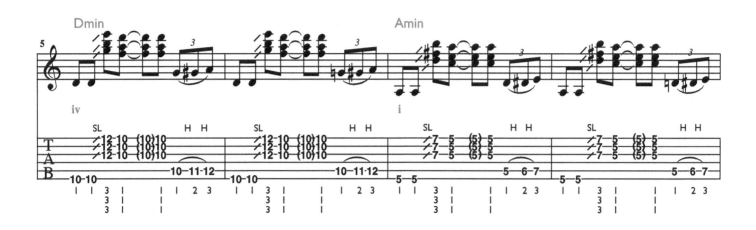

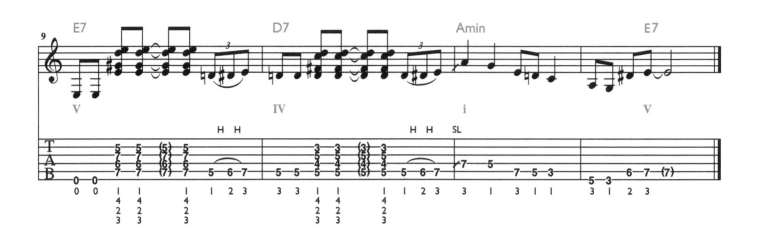

Here, we'll hammer-on from a ♭3 to a ♮3, turning a minor triad into a major triad.

HAMMER-ON TRIAD BLUES

Track 37

Now that we've covered major and minor triads on the top three strings, let's move on to the more common dominant 7th chords on the top four strings. Practice the following E7, A7 and B7 voicings. Be sure to learn and play these shapes all over the fretboard.

E7 Voicings

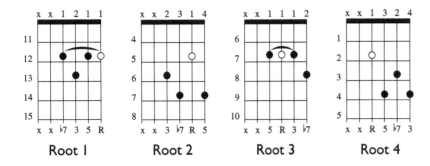

A7 Voicings

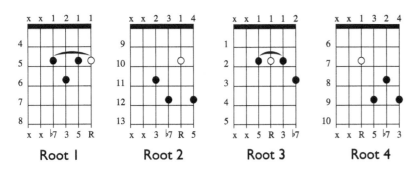

B7 Voicings

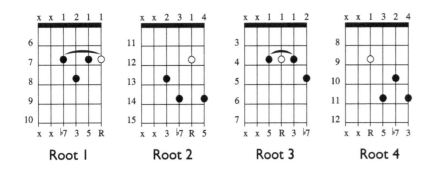

This next piece uses various dominant 7th shapes up and down the fretboard.

DOMINANT 7TH BLUES

Track 38

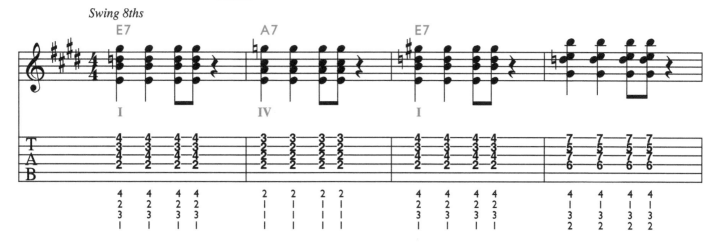

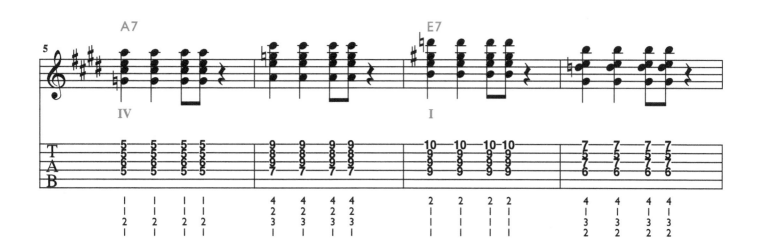

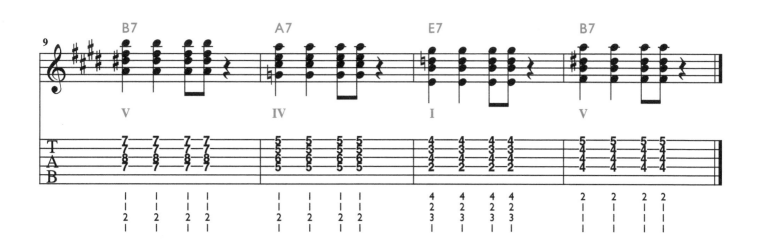

This piece in $\frac{12}{8}$ time has a popular right-hand rhythmic pattern. Play it with a pick or use your fingers. Fingerstyle players use the Spanish terms for the right-hand fingers: *pulgar* for thumb, *indice* for index, *medio* for middle and *anular* for the ring finger. These are abbreviated as *p*, *i*, *m* and *a*. We will be doing more with fingerstyle technique in Chapter 12 (Open Tunings, page 157) and Chapter 14 (More Fingerstyle Blues, page 163). The I–IV–I–V progression in the last two measures is a classic blues ending.

BLUES IN $\frac{12}{8}$

Track 39

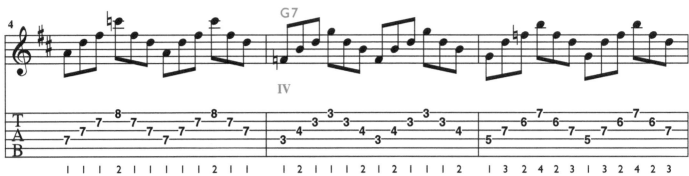

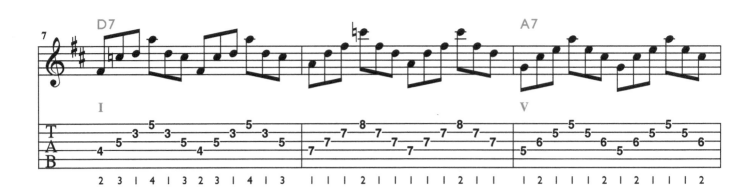

CHAPTER 7

Boogie Woogie Blues

In *Beginning Acoustic Blues Guitar*, we learned that *boogie woogie* is a blues piano style in which a pianist usually plays a steady eighth-note pattern with the left hand, and chords and melody with the right hand. The eighth-note pattern, which is based on the major scale, usually proceeds from the tonic, to the 3, to the 5, then to the 6 and/or $\flat$7. This pattern is played ascending and then descending (for example, 1–3–5–6–$\flat$7–6–5–3, etc.).

Not only are boogie woogie patterns fun to play on guitar, it's also fun to say, "I play boogie woogie blues guitar." In this style, guitar players imitate the left-hand patterns of boogie woogie pianists.

In this chapter, we'll take our standard boogie woogie patterns and spice them up by adding new riffs and techniques. The pieces you'll learn will sound great by themselves, but even better with a chord accompaniment. So get a friend and have fun playing through these variations.

PHOTO COURTESY INSTITUTE OF JAZZ STUDIES, RUTGERS UNIVERSITY

*Boogie woogie piano music inspired **Huddie "Leadbelly" Ledbetter** (1888–1949) to become a musician. Discovered while serving a prison sentence in Louisiana, he achieved fame in the 1940s. Two of his most popular recordings, "Midnight Special" and "Goodnight, Irene," have been covered by many artists.*

This piece has a group of four sixteenth notes on the third beat of each measure (except the last). They take the place of the two eighth notes that usually occupy that spot. This simple change adds some excitement to the music. Pick all the eighth notes with downstrokes, but use alternating picking for the sixteenth notes.

 SIXTEENTH-NOTE BOOGIE WOOGIE

Track 40

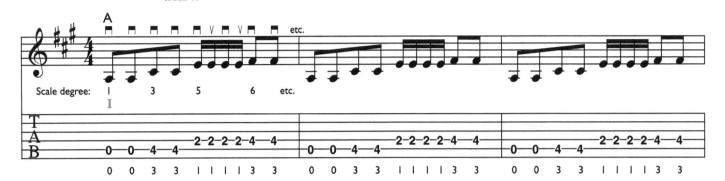

Scale degree: 1   3   5   6   etc.

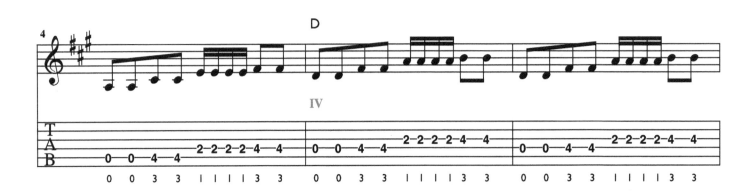

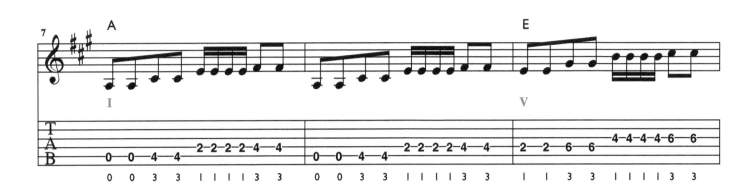

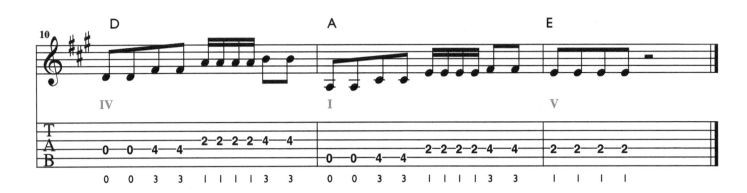

Most boogie woogie patterns start by moving from the 1 to the 3 of a major scale. In the tune below, we move from the 1 to our classic ♭3 to ♮3 (G♮ to G♯), which gives this type of pattern a very strong sound when played on the lower strings. Although most boogie woogie patterns ascend and descend with the same notes, this one takes a twist in the second bar and adds a ♭7 (D).

♭3 BOOGIE WOOGIE IN E

Track 41

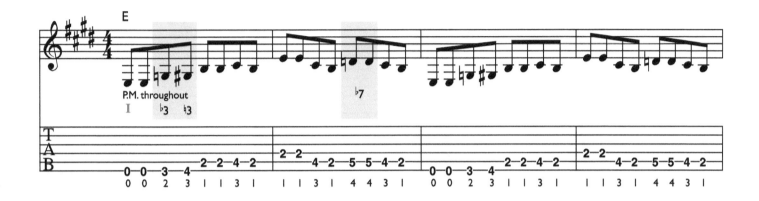

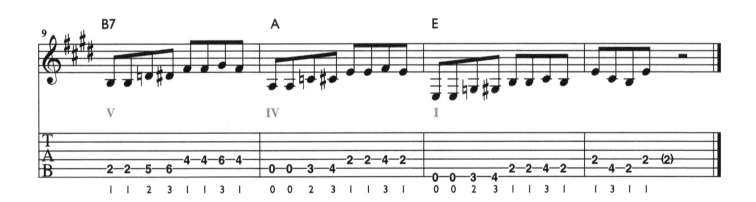

This next piece, in the key of F, is based on a one-bar boogie woogie riff. Like the example on page 135, it also has a ♭3 (A♭) moving to a ♮3 (A♮). This time, however, we'll hammer-on to the ♮3. The triplets on the second and fourth beats give this a swinging sound.

♭3 BOOGIE WOOGIE IN F

Track 42

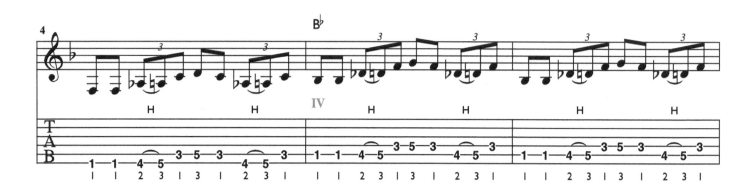

CHAPTER 8

Intervals

As you learned on page 26, an interval is the distance in pitch between two notes. Let's take a closer look at intervals.

By counting the note names between two notes, we get a number name. For example, the letter C is three letters away from E. So, the interval from C to E is a third (3rd).

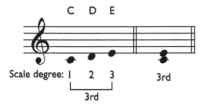

That sounds easy enough, but what would you call a C♯ and E? Or a C and E♭? Their musical distance is different than C and E, so they have to be distinguished from the 3rd in the above example. We solve this problem by *qualifying* the number with the terms *major (M)*, *minor (m)*, *perfect (P)* and *diminished (d)*.

The examples on page 138 illustrate the thirteen intervals—all starting with the C note—within one octave. Play them *harmonically* (together) and *melodically* (in succession) to familiarize yourself with how they sound. Then, play all of them with different starting notes.

Intervals can be described as *consonant* or *dissonant*. A consonant interval is one that sounds stable or resolved—some would say "sweet" or "pleasant." Thirds (3rds) and *sixths (6ths)* (see page 138) fall into this category. Intervals that are *not* consonant are described as dissonant. They create musical tension and can sound harsh and unresolved. Traditionally, dissonant intervals sound best when they resolve to consonant intervals. The *minor 2nd* and *diminished 5th* (see page 138) are examples of dissonance.

As you study intervals give special attention to the 3rds and 6ths. As you will see in Chapter 9 (starting on page 139), they are often used in acoustic blues pieces to harmonize melodies and enhance accompaniment patterns.

The Intervals

Track 43

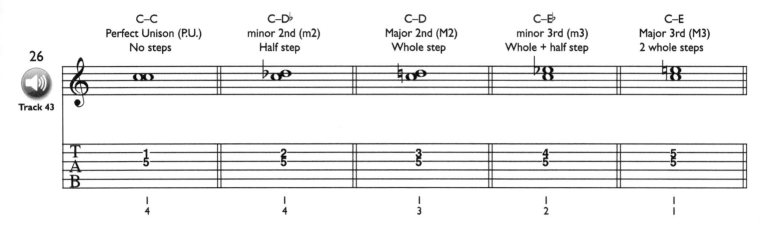

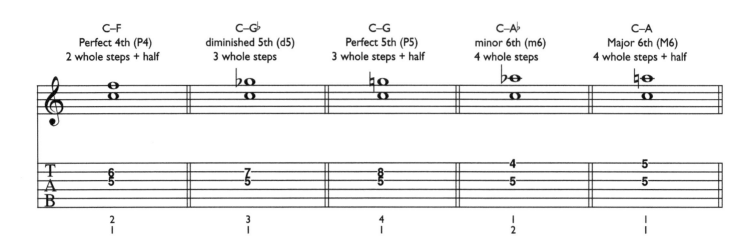

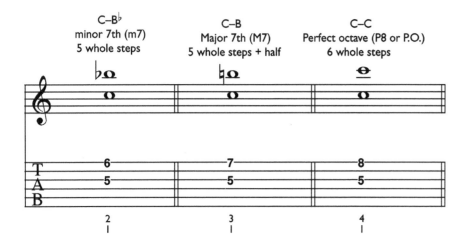

CHAPTER 9

3rds, 6ths and 10ths

Blues players often use 3rds, 6ths and 10ths—the consonant intervals—in solos and accompaniments. The first part of this chapter will help you to understand these sounds. The musical examples at the end will show you how great they sound when used in a blues context.

3RDS

In Chapter 8 (pages 137 and 138), we saw there are two types of 3rds—major and minor. A major 3rd consists of two whole steps; a minor 3rd consists of one whole step plus a half step. When we *harmonize* a scale or melody, we are adding additional notes and playing them simultaneously with the original notes. If we harmonize a major scale in 3rds, we'll wind up with a particular sequence of major and minor 3rds. Let's see how this works by first looking at the C Major scale.

C Major Scale

27

Track 44

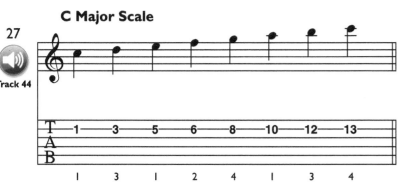

Now let's harmonize the scale in 3rds. We'll add the third note (E) to the first note (C). The notes C and E are a major 3rd apart. Now we'll add an F to the second note, D. These two notes are one-and-a-half steps apart, so they produce the interval of a minor 3rd. When we harmonize the major scale in 3rds, we will naturally have some major and some minor 3rds. The diagrams (below right) show you the fingerings for these intervals. The musical example will demonstrate the entire scale in 3rds.

C Major Scale Harmonized in 3rds

28

Track 45

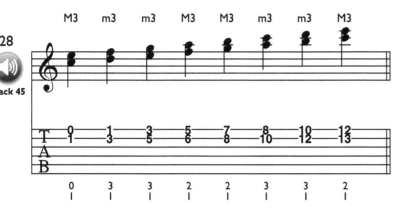

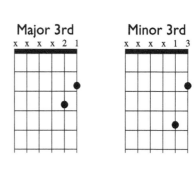

It's true that the major scale harmonized in 3rds can be used to produce a "sweet" and pleasant sound. However, blues players are not always shooting for sweet and pleasant. We like it a little harsher and funkier. This can be accomplished by going outside of diatonic harmony. The songs toward the end of this chapter (starting on page 142) will show you how this is often done in a blues setting.

6THS

When harmonizing a scale in 3rds, we added a new note *above* the original scale tone. When harmonizing in 6ths, we'll add a note *below* the original. Whether harmonizing in 3rds or in 6ths, it is the same note we are adding, just in a different octave. Three scale degrees up from C gives us an E, six scale degrees *down* also gives us an E.

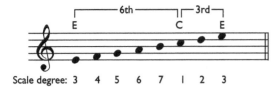

This is why 6ths share a consonant sound with 3rds. You can play the following scale—harmonized in 6ths—fingerstyle or with *hybrid picking*. Hybrid picking is a style that integrates the use of a pick with fingerstyle. In the case below, you'd play the lower note of the 6th with a pick and the upper note with your middle finger. The shapes for these 6ths are shown under the musical example.

C Major Scale Harmonized in 6ths

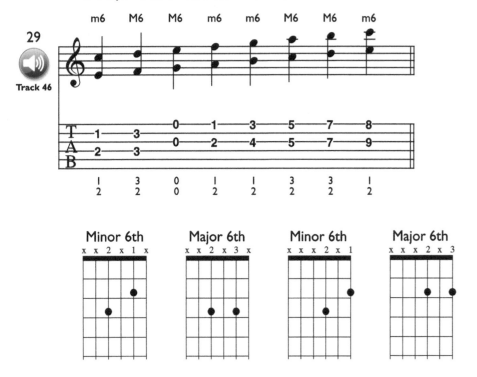

10THS

We know that the distance between the notes C and E is a major 3rd. Well, what happens when we go from C to the *next* E in the scale? This second E is one octave higher than the first, and since it is ten notes away from our starting C it's called a *10th*. All 10ths share the same two notes as their corresponding 3rds. They have a similar tonal quality but are much *wider* intervals. For example:

Below is the C Major scale harmonized in 10ths. To play it, you can use fingerstyle or hybrid picking. Notice that the order of the interval qualities—major (M) and minor (m)—are the same as with the 3rds.

C Major Scale Harmonized in 10ths

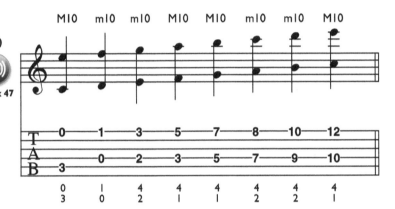

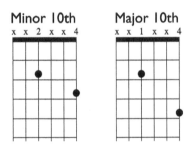

When playing 10ths on guitar, the original scale tone is on the lower strings and the new note is on the upper strings. For this reason, 10ths are often used in fingerstyle. This wide interval produces a full, chord-like sound, and can be easily integrated into a melody. The guitar part to "Blackbird," by The Beatles, is largely based on this sound.

3RDS, 6THS AND 10THS IN BLUES STYLE

Now that we've taken a close look at 3rds, 6ths and 10ths, we can look at how they are used in a blues context. To do this, we'll have to step outside of diatonic harmony. When we harmonized the C Major scale, we showed all the diatonic 3rds, 6ths and 10ths in the key of C. However, all the harmonized scales included the 3rds and 7ths that naturally occur in the major scale. Since this is not a scale that is used in the blues, we need to alter some notes to get a blues sound. Of course, we'll have to flat the 3s and 7s (giving us minor 3rds and minor 7ths) to achieve the correct tonalities.

3RDS IN BLUES STYLE

The next two examples—in the popular key of E—include the most commonly used patterns for 3rds on the upper strings. The G-naturals are ♭3s in the key of E, and in this context produce minor 3rds where, in diatonic harmony, they would be major 3rds. The D-naturals are ♭7s and produce minor 7ths where, in diatonic harmony, they would be major 7ths. Note, however, that the first beat in the second bar of example 31 has a ♮3 (G♯). This is standard practice when playing 3rds on the 2nd and 3rd strings. It gives us a phrase contrasting the ♭3 with the ♮3, and enables us to keep the same minor 3rd shape as you move up the fretboard. You will, however, need to use both major and minor 3rd shapes for example 32.

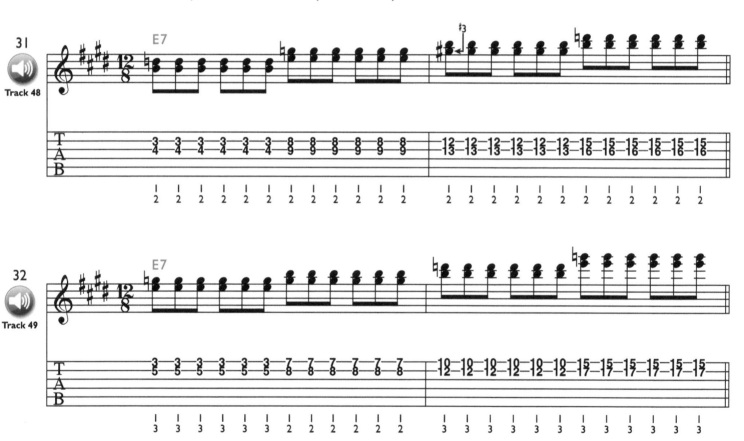

The solo below incorporates 3rds with single-note scale licks. The minor 3rd that begins the sixth bar is part of an A7 chord, and the one in the ninth bar is part of a B7. There is a quarter-step bend on the bottom note of the 3rd in bar 3. This raises the pitch to a sound between the ♭3 (G♮) and ♮3 (G♯), which produces a real bluesy feel. Learn this piece and then start to add 3rds to your own solos. This solo sounds great when played over a honky tonk accompaniment. Be sure to check this out on the recording.

SOLO WITH 3RDS

Track 50

6THS IN BLUES STYLE

This next tune has a popular blues move—sliding 6ths on the second beat of almost every measure. The turnaround is based on a D *Augmented chord*. Augmented (Aug or +) chords consist of the following chord tones: 1–3–#5. Fret the notes of this chord simultaneously and let the notes sustain as you play them.

SLIDING 6TH BLUES

Track 51

This piece is similar to two-string shuffles we've already covered, with the exception that we're using 6th shapes with added open strings for a fuller sound. Strum it with a pick or your thumb, but be sure to mute all the strings marked with an x in the chord diagrams.

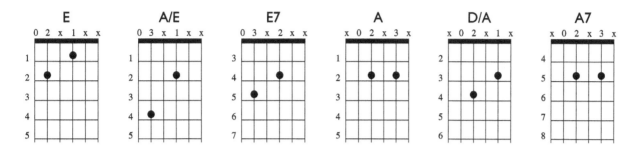

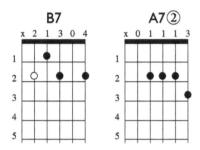

SHUFFLIN' 6THS

Track 52

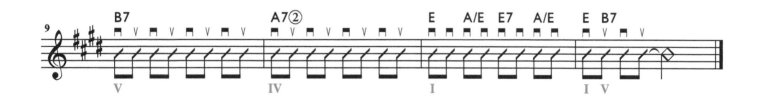

10THS IN BLUES STYLE

Our next example is composed entirely of 10ths. It's in the style of Robert Lockwood Jr., who learned his craft first-hand from the great Robert Johnson. You can use hybrid picking, but it will probably sound better if you play the low notes with your thumb *(p)* and upper notes with your index *(i)* and/or middle finger *(m)*.

BLUES IN 10THS

Track 53

CHAPTER 10

Arpeggios

An *arpeggio* is the notes of a chord played individually, rather than simultaneously. Arpeggios are a great option to keep in mind when soloing. Learn all the arpeggios in this chapter and add them to your "bag of tricks." Note that many keys are used in the following examples. The reason for this is that you should be familiar with these arpeggios in any key.

MAJOR ARPEGGIOS

Major arpeggios consist of chord tones: 1–3–5. Below is an A Major arpeggio (A–C♯–E). Like the rest of the arpeggios in this chapter, it's a movable shape. This means you can turn it into any major arpeggio you like. For example, move it up a whole step and you have a B Major arpeggio; move it down a whole step and you have a G Major arpeggio.

A Major Arpeggio

There is only one note in this example that is *not* in the A Major arpeggio—the F♯ in the last bar.

MINOR ARPEGGIOS

Minor arpeggios consist of chord tones: 1–♭3–5. Here is an A Minor arpeggio (A–C–E).

A Minor Arpeggio

This example starts with G Minor arpeggio patterns, but ends with a pentatonic figure.

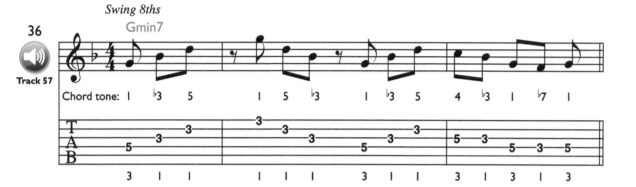

DOMINANT 7TH ARPEGGIOS

Dominant 7th arpeggios consist of chord tones: 1–3–5–♭7. Below is an A Dominant 7th (A7) arpeggio (A–C♯–E–G♮).

A Dominant 7th Arpeggio

The example below is based on the A7 arpeggio.

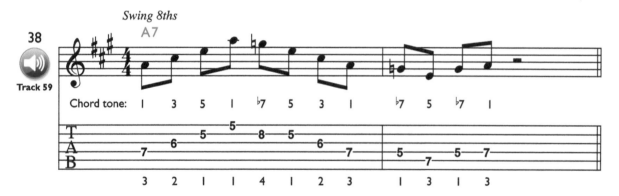

There are many different fingerings for arpeggios. Discover your own and make them part of your soloing vocabulary. Below is another movable dominant 7th arpeggio fingering. This one is a D7 arpeggio (D–F#–A–C#).

D Dominant 7th Arpeggio

This example in D consists entirely of notes from the dominant 7th arpeggio. A cool sound is produced by ending on the ♭7.

MINOR 7TH ARPEGGIOS

If you flat the 3rd of a dominant 7th arpeggio, you get a *minor 7th* arpeggio. The chord tones are: 1–♭3–5–♭7. Below, we have an A Minor 7th—or Amin7—arpeggio (A–C–E–G).

A Minor 7th Arpeggio

We are using a Bmin7 arpeggio for this next example.

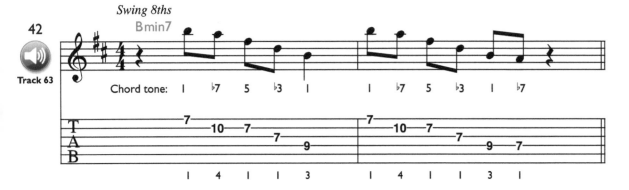

MAJOR 6TH ARPEGGIOS

A *major 6th* chord is a major triad with a 6th on top. We'll be covering these chords in *Mastering Acoustic Blues Guitar*. Since, however, the major 6th arpeggio is used often in *jump blues* (an up-tempo jazz-style blues), we'll include it here as well. Its chord tones are: 1–3–5–6. Below is an arpeggio for an A Major 6th, or A6, arpeggio (A–C#–E–F#).

A Major 6th Arpeggio

B♭ is one of the most popular keys for jump blues. A reason for this is that horn players find it an easy key in which to play—and trumpets and saxophones are crucial to this style. Let's try this cool jump-style example.

CHAPTER 11

9th, 13th and Diminished 7th Chords

The dominant 7th chord is essential to the blues sound, but to add some variety to your playing, you'll need to know other types of chords as well. The chords in this chapter are a little more sophisticated than the basic dominant 7th chord; they'll help you achieve a more "jazzy" sounding blues.

DOMINANT 9TH CHORDS

As you well know, dominant 7th chords consist of $1-3-5-{}^{\flat}7$. A *dominant 9th* chord is produced by adding a 9 to a dominant 7th chord. The 9 is the same note as the 2, but it is usually placed in a higher octave. We'll also include the *dominant 7♯9* chord. Here, the 9 is raised a half step. The 9th chord is a blues classic and the 7♯9 is a fun and funky chord used extensively by Jimi Hendrix, Stevie Ray Vaughan and many other artists. To the right are two movable forms—one for an E Dominant 9th chord and the other for an E Dominant 7th ♯9.

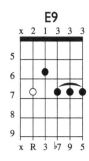

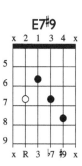

DOMINANT 13TH CHORDS

For our 13th chord, we'll once again start with a dominant 7th and we'll add a 13 to it. This note is the same as the 6 in the major scale, but again, it would be in a higher octave. To the right is a standard root-6 shape for a dominant 13th chord.

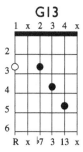

DIMINISHED 7TH CHORDS

A *diminished 7th* (dim7 or °7) chord consists of $1-{}^{\flat}3-{}^{\flat}5-{}^{\flat\flat}7$. Notice that the 7 is preceded by two flat signs (♭♭). This is a *double flat* and tells us to lower the 7 two half steps, or a whole step. The ♭♭7 is an enharmonic equivalent of the 6 in the major scale, which means they sound and are played exactly the same. Since each note is a minor 3rd away from its neighbor, any note can be considered the root. So, if you move the form up three frets you wind up with all the same chord tones—hence, the same chord, just voiced differently. The diminished 7th is one of our most dissonant chords and is used as a colorful transition between other chords or parts of a tune. For the purposes of the illustrations to the right, the lowest note is indicated as the root.

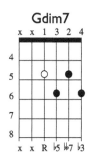

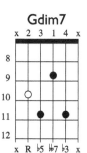

Be sure to keep the strums short and choppy in this next one. The ending is a classic in both blues and early rock 'n' roll music.

9TH CHORD BLUES IN G

Track 66

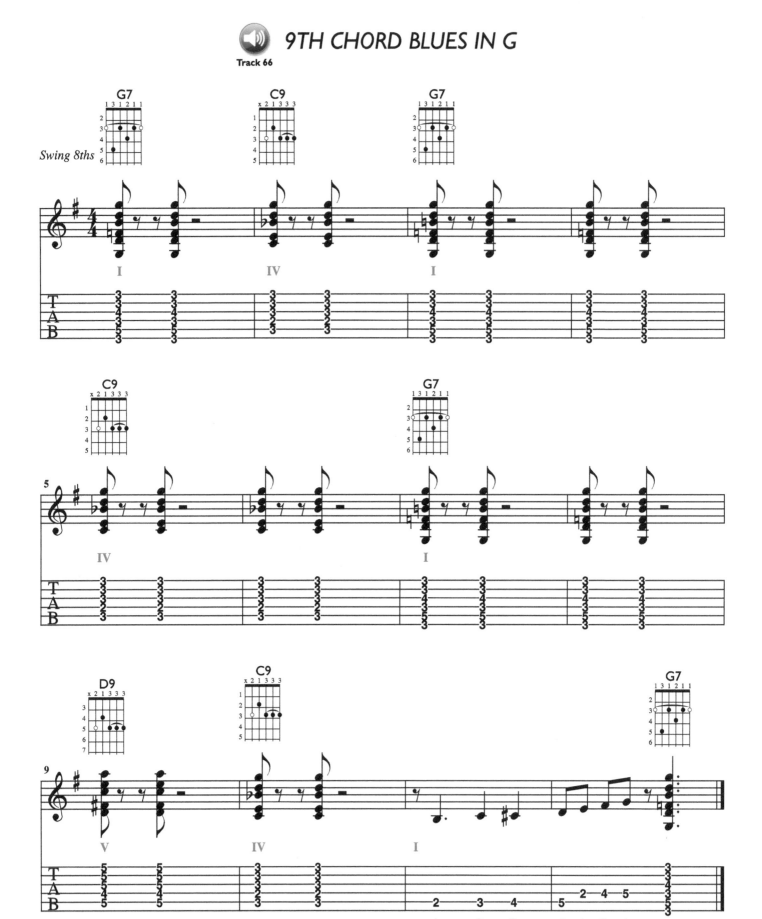

Our next piece combines a cool riff with dominant 13th and 7#9 chords. Watch the hammer-ons and slides and have fun with this funky soul/blues tune.

FUNKY BLUES IN E

Track 67

Sliding in half steps from one 9th or 13th chord to another is a common move. This approach is used in the tune below. Maintain pressure with your left-hand fingers throughout the slide or the notes will stop sounding.

13TH CHORD BLUES

Track 68

"Diminished 7th Blues" features a mix of dominant and diminished 7th chords. The chord names in gray indicate what kind of chord or arpeggio you are playing. Hold your fingers in place so that all the notes ring out.

Track 69

DIMINISHED 7TH BLUES

Chapter 11—9th, 13th and Diminished 7th Chords   155

The blues is an essential part of jazz. Check out this "Jazz Blues." It is based on a 12-bar blues and includes a VI–II–V–I pattern and a ♯iv diminished 7th chord in bar 6. We'll cover more advanced jazz blues concepts in the *Mastering* section.

Track 70

JAZZ BLUES

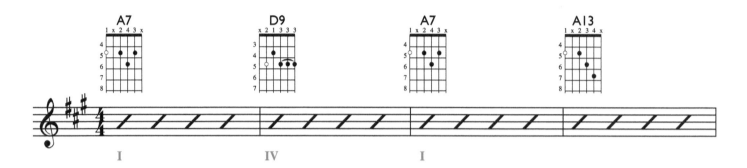

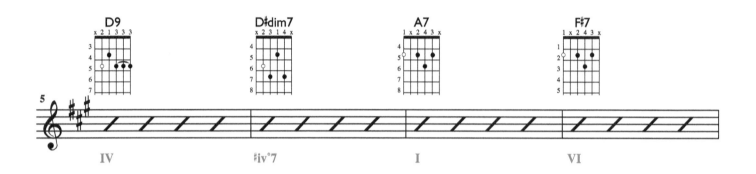

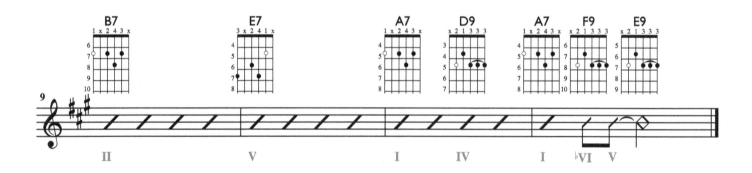

CHAPTER 12

Open Tunings

Most of the early blues greats used *open tunings,* in which the open strings are tuned to form a major or minor chord. In this chapter, we'll look at the tunings: *open G, open A, open D* and *open E.*

OPEN G TUNING

From the 6th string to the 1st, the strings in *open G tuning* are tuned: D–G–D–G–B–D. This is sometimes called Spanish tuning, even though the vast repertoire of Spanish folk, flamenco and classical styles are based on standard tuning. In open G tuning, the 2nd, 3rd and 4th strings are the same as in standard tuning; the others are tuned lower.

To tune to open G, you can use a *chromatic tuner* (an electronic tuner that allows you to tune to any note), or you can follow this method:

1. Play the 6th string, 7th fret and lower it until it matches the open 5th string.
2. Play the open 5th string and lower it until it matches the 6th string, 5th fret.
3. Play the open 1st string and lower it until it matches the 2nd string, 3rd fret.

Below are some common chords in open G tuning. Learn them and use your voluminous blues knowledge to compose your own blues tune in G.

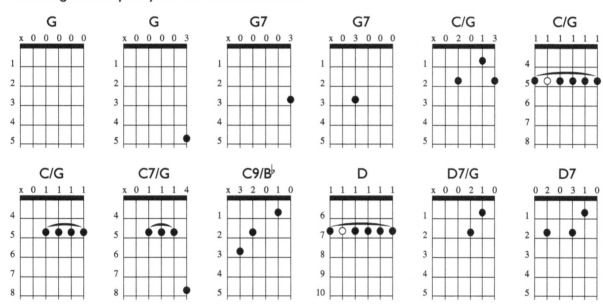

FINGERSTYLE REVIEW

Fingerstyle is the standard approach for playing in open tunings. To the right is a list of the Spanish names and abbreviations for the right-hand fingers. Traditionally, the thumb *(p)* is assigned to the notes on the lower three strings; in standard music notation, the stems for these notes point downward. The index *(i)*, middle *(m)* and ring *(a)* fingers are assigned to the top three strings; the stems for these notes point upward. When there are two or more notes on the upper strings, try sounding them both by brushing upward with your index finger. This will give you a rougher blues sound and is indicated in the music with the symbol ⌡.

Right-Hand Fingers
- *pulgar (p)* for thumb
- *indice (i)* for index
- *medio (m)* for middle
- *anular (a)* for ring

If you are unfamiliar with fingerstyle technique, it may be helpful for you to review the Fingerstyle Blues chapter in the first book of this series, or *Beginning Fingerstyle Guitar* (Manzi) published by Alfred Music #14099.

"Blues in Open G" features some of the most popular licks for this tuning. The figure in the 4th bar is similar to phrases in Robert Johnson's music. Notice that, in this book, the new note names for all the strings in an open tuning are at the beginning of each TAB staff.

BLUES IN OPEN G

Track 71

Rests can also be dotted. In $\frac{12}{8}$ time, a *dotted quarter rest* gets 3 beats of silence (2 + 1 = 3).

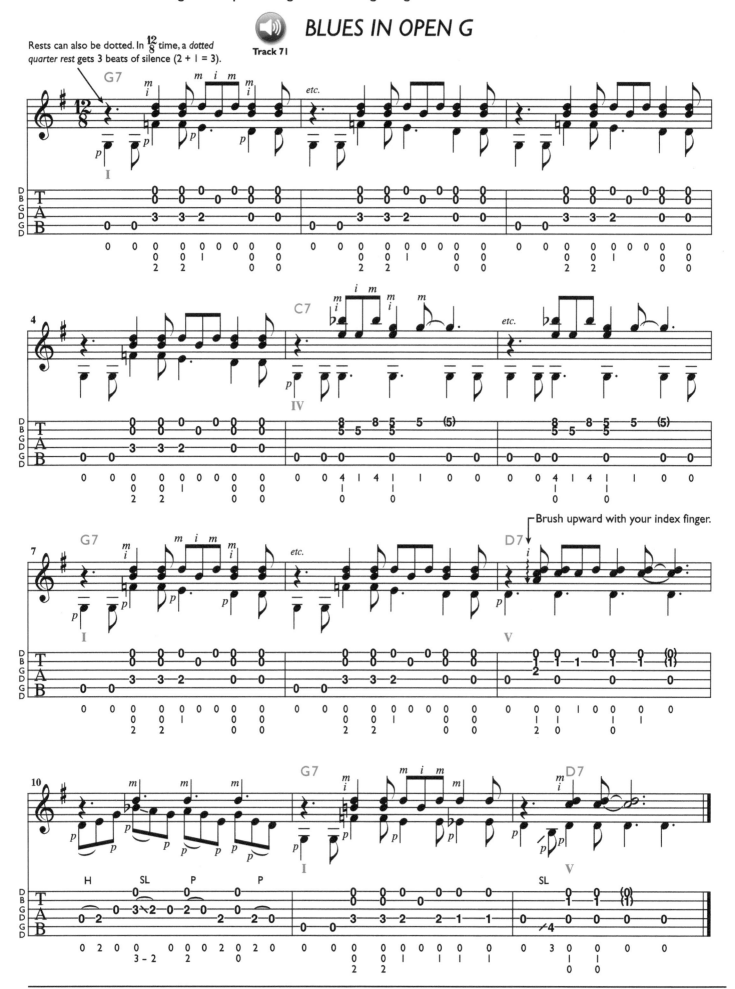

OPEN A TUNING

From the 6th to the 1st string, the strings in *open A tuning* are tuned: E–A–E–A–C#–E. The 1st, 5th and 6th strings stay the same as in standard tuning, and the others are *raised* to form the notes of an A chord. The string relationships in this tuning are the same as in open G, but each note is a whole step higher. Every chord and phrase can be played the same way as in open G, but the sound would be brighter. Another way to achieve this sound is to stay in open G and place a *capo* (device that wraps around the fretboard to raise the pitch of the strings) on the 2nd fret. For now, just tune your guitar to open A and play "Blues in Open G" (page 158) by reading the tablature exactly as written. Again, the tune will be the same, with all the musical relationships intact, but it will just sound a little higher and brighter.

OPEN D TUNING

From the 6th string to the 1st, the strings in *open D tuning* are tuned: D–A–D–F#–A–D. In this tuning, we can exploit the low-D string, which is the root of the I chord. This gives open D tuning a very strong sound. The early country blues players often called it "Vastapol" or "Sebastopol" tuning, after a popular song from the mid-1800s written in this tuning.

You can tune to open D by using a chromatic tuner, or by using the following method:
1. Play the 7th fret, 6th string and lower it until it matches the open 5th string.
2. Lower the 3rd string until it matches the 4th string, 4th fret.
3. Lower the 2nd string until it matches the 3rd string, 3rd fret.
4. Lower the 1st string until it matches the 2nd string, 5th fret.

Play around with the following chords and you'll start to hear the sounds of the *Delta blues* (one of the earliest forms of the blues, from the Mississippi Delta region).

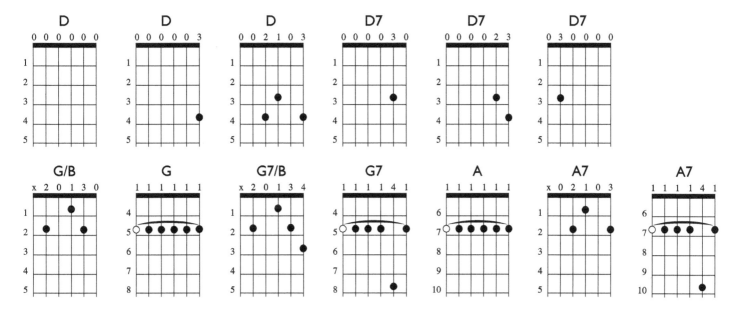

Our next piece, "Open D Blues" (page 160) features many popular "moves" used in this tuning. In most of the measures, your thumb should forcefully strum downward, hitting the two lowest strings. The double stops on the upper strings should be strummed upward with the index finger. The piece ends with a common open D turnaround.

OPEN E TUNING

Open E tuning has the same string relationships as open D, but each string is one whole step higher: E–B–E–G♯–B–E. Placing a capo on the 2nd fret in open D will give you the same notes as open E. For now, try tuning to open E and playing the "Open D Blues" above, following the TAB rather than the standard music notation. The music will sound the same, just a little higher in pitch.

CHAPTER 13

Boogie Blues

Boogie blues—not to be confused with boogie *woogie* blues (Chapter 7, page 133)—is a choppy, percussive and exciting approach to rhythm guitar. If you've heard John Lee Hooker, then you've heard the master of guitar boogie. You'll also hear boogie style tunes in the music of ZZ Top, Canned Heat and George Thorogood.

Guitar boogies are basically one chord *vamps*. A vamp is a repetitive accompaniment figure or phrase. Other chords may be used in passing, but there is always a quick return to the I chord. It's also common to leave the I chord to play some single-note fills, usually from the minor pentatonic scale.

Our first boogie blues example is based on an A chord, "A" being the most common boogie key. Strum the chord up (∨) on the offbeats (&s), and tap the strings with the pinky-side of your right hand on the onbeats (the numbers). Tap lightly, but enough to hear the sound of the strings hitting the fretboard and your hand tapping the guitar body. We are looking for a percussive tap followed by an upstrum on the chord. The drum-like tap is notated with the symbol ×. Using your right-hand index finger for the strums will give you a great blues sound, but you could also use a pick.

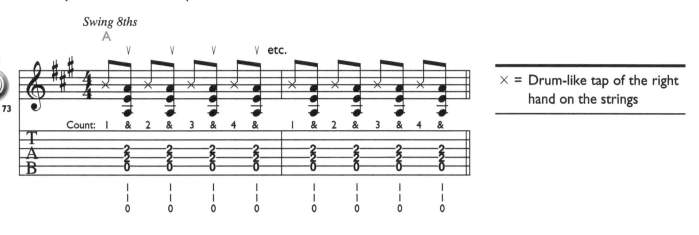

× = Drum-like tap of the right hand on the strings

In the example below, ♭III (C/A) and IV (D/A) chords are quickly thrown in for excitement. Give special attention to the double-stop hammer-on in bars 2 to 3—from the open 3rd and 4th strings back to the A chord. This, in combination with the chuck-strum technique explained above, gives to the boogie its characteristic bounce and snap.

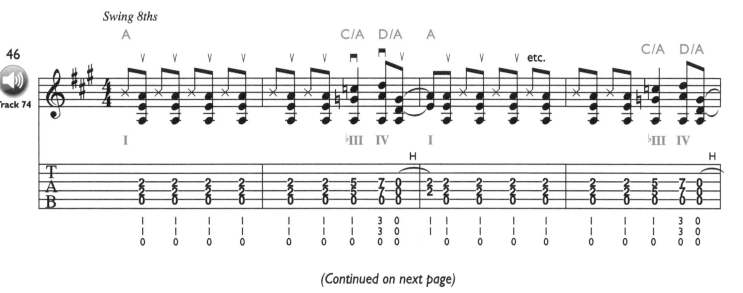

(Continued on next page)

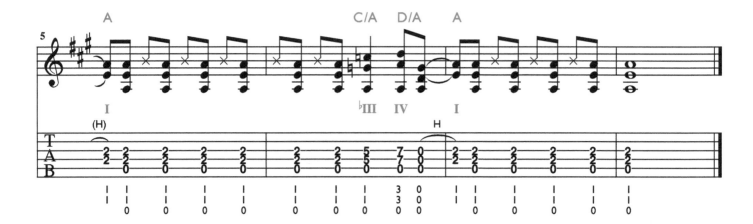

Now we'll change our rhythm slightly and add a melodic fill. As mentioned before, most boogie style licks are from the minor pentatonic scale. Practice moving from the I chord to your own solo licks and back again.

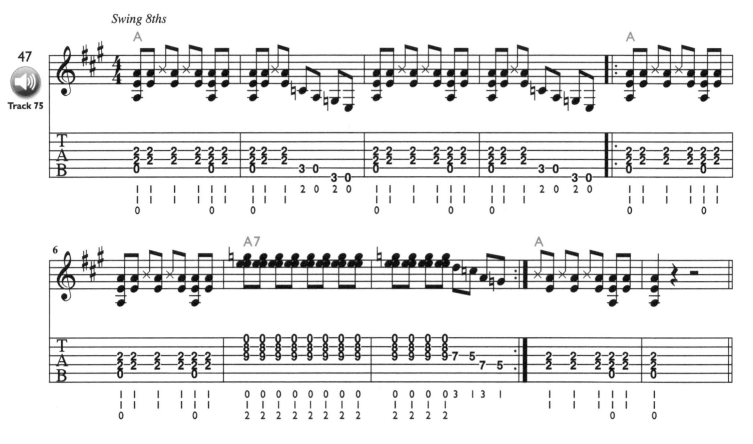

The key of E is another popular boogie key. Add some E Minor Pentatonic scale licks to this example, put on your dark sunglasses and you can be John Lee Hooker for the day.

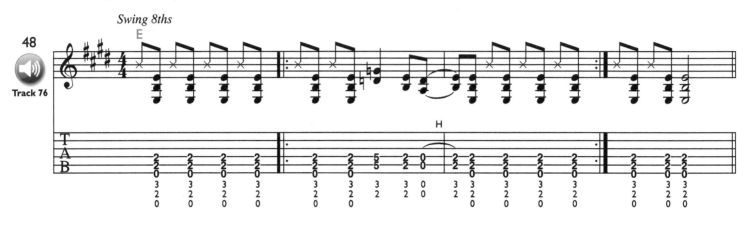

CHAPTER 14

More Fingerstyle Blues

Fingerstyle has been offered as an option throughout this book. The Open Tunings chapter (page 157) was exclusively for this technique. The five pieces in this section are in the most common fingerstyle keys: A, C, D, E and G. Some use a *monotonic bass* pattern, where the bass notes (played by the thumb) consist only of a chord's root notes. Some are in *alternating bass* style, where the bass notes alternate between two notes on the lower strings. A boogie woogie bass pattern is also thrown into the mix. Your studies from this book and the first in the series come to fruition in these pieces.

"Blues for Robert" combines a monotonic bass pattern with double stops and triads on the upper strings. It's in the style of the great Robert Johnson.

BLUES FOR ROBERT

Track 77

(Continued on next page)

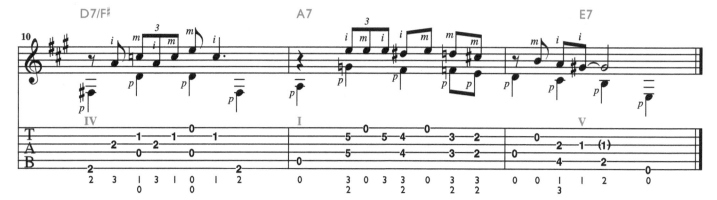

This next piece is in *drop D tuning*. This is an *altered tuning,* which is any tuning *other* than *standard tuning* (E–A–D–G–B–E). Although all open tunings are considered to be alternate tunings, drop D is not an open tuning because the open strings do not form a major or minor chord. In drop D, only one string is changed—the 6th string is lowered to D. This can be achieved by, 1) Using a tuner, or, 2) Playing the 6th string, 7th fret and lowering it to match the open 5th string. Notice the alternating bass used throughout this piece, and the use of 3rds at the beginning and 6ths at the end.

DROP D BLUES

Track 78

The hammer-on from the ♭3 (G♮) to the ♮3 (G♯) is a classic fingerstyle move in the key of E.
Watch the slides up to the A7 chord in bars 5 and 6, you'll need to barre these notes with
your 1st finger. This is in the style of Mance Lipscomb's "Sugar Babe."

BLUES FOR MANCE

This piece is in the style of Blind Lemon Jefferson. Bars 1, 2, 3 and 7 suggest a C chord sound, but do not try to hold onto a C fingering; these measures feature melodic passages and are not intended as C chord accompaniment patterns. The other bars, however, *are* based on particular chord fingerings. Don't forget, when you see an *i* accompanied by ⌡, strum the chord tones by lightly brushing upward with your right-hand 1st finger. We end with a cool sequence of descending 3rds.

BLIND LEMON BLUES

Track 80

Swing 8ths

This piece combines a boogie woogie bass line (see page 133, Boogie Woogie Blues) with melodic licks on the upper strings. Practice it bar-by-bar until you really get it under your fingers. Be sure to hold the bass notes for their full value. When you've got it down, try to add new variations over the same bass part.

BOOGIE WOOGIE IN G

Track 81

FINAL THOUGHTS

Before diving into the *Mastering* section, I'd like to pause for a moment and consider some of the great blues masters. I've always been deeply moved by the music of Leadbelly, Lightnin' Hopkins, Ry Cooder, Mississippi John Hurt, Howlin' Wolf and Muddy Waters. The late Dave Van Ronk was also a strong influence on me, with his ability to move from style to style and make each his own.

The one thing all the great masters have in common is a lifetime of devotion to the music. Yes, it's fun to play guitar, it's a good way to spend some time either by yourself or with friends. But if you want to be a real blues musician, you have to be *committed* to your musical growth. You should play and practice enough to continually move ahead and learn new things. The more you learn, the better you'll feel about yourself as a player.

Go over and over the material in this book—until you have it down cold. It takes many repetitions to really lock into new chords, scales and techniques. But don't stop there. It's important for you to make your *own* music. Try to play standard progressions in new ways. Create your own licks and riffs. Compose your own blues tunes, using what you've learned while making your way through these chapters. Whether you play at a famous blues club or in your friend's basement, you'll enjoy it more when you express yourself in your own unique way.

If you've made it through most of the music in the first two sections of this book, you're ready to play out. If you've already been doing this, you know how good it makes you feel. If you have not yet started, here's a plan:

1. Pick a few of your favorite blues songs and practice singing and playing them (or find a friend who can sing while you play). It's always more fun to play with other people. Maybe you want to join forces with another guitarist and really start jamming.
2. As soon as you can run through a few songs, find some open mics and play for an audience.
3. Keep adding to your set list, and then do a full set at a coffee house or local club.

I've seen many people make the transition from playing at home to playing in public, and although it can be scary, no one seems to regret it. Don't forget about venues like community centers, nursing homes, schools and anywhere else you can find groups of people. Some folks just like to play for themselves. That's okay, but most of us feel that preparing for public performances really helps us improve as players.

I would, of course, encourage you to move on to the *Mastering* section, which features many more fingerpicking pieces in the styles of the early country blues masters. We'll take a much deeper look at open tunings, and get into some bottleneck slide as well. It also includes advanced soloing techniques, jazz blues, modes and improvising over the entire fretboard.

If you have any questions or comments you can get in touch with me at: loumanzi@snet.net. Thanks for taking the time to work your way through this book and *have fun playing the blues!*

MASTERING
ACOUSTIC
BLUES GUITAR

Audio tracks recorded by Jason Alborough at WorkshopLive.com, Pittsfield, MA

TABLE OF CONTENTS

ABOUT THIS BOOK

If you've made it to this section, you should already have some good acoustic blues chops under your belt, and you want to continue to take your playing to higher levels. In this section, you will learn new techniques and tunes, and be introduced to concepts that will make you a force to be reckoned with on the acoustic blues scene.

To get the most out of the next section, you should already know how to read standard music notation and tablature (TAB), and have a good understanding of chord and scale theory. It's true that you don't need to be a classically trained composer and theorist to play the blues, but if you have a good grasp on the basic ideas and language of music, it can only help you to be a better player.

In this section, we'll take a much deeper look at fingerpicking blues styles, with many pieces in open and alternate tunings. Also, since slide or bottleneck playing is a vital part of the blues sound, we'll take a good look at this exciting style.

You'll learn new progressions with more variations than the standard three-chord 12-bar blues. You'll also learn new "jazzy" fingerings for popular blues chords. The chapters on soloing and modes offer new approaches to improvising. We'll look at all the important scale fingerings used in blues, cover new soloing concepts and explain how the great players combine different scales to create exciting and masterful solos.

You don't have to go through this section page-by-page. It may be more interesting for you to work on a few pages from different chapters simultaneously—or just dig in deep to particular chapters that appeal to you the most. *Really listen* to the accompanying recording. It will help you to get the proper feel of the examples in ways that the notation or TAB alone cannot.

You can spend a lifetime learning to play the blues. It's a great style that allows us to express a wide range of emotions, from exuberant joy to deep sadness. We hope that working through the following material will be a rewarding experience for you, and that it will help you to create your own original blues music. It's a long and rewarding road—be creative and enjoy every step along the way.

00

Track 1

Online audio is included with this book to make learning easier and more enjoyable. The symbol shown on the left appears next to every example in the book that features an audio track. Use the recordings to ensure you're capturing the feel of the examples and interpreting the rhythms correctly. The track number below the symbol corresponds directly to the example you want to hear (example numbers are above the icon). All the track numbers are unique to each "book" within this volume, meaning every book has its own Track 1, Track 2, and so on. (For example, *Beginning Acoustic Blues Guitar* starts with Track 1, as does *Intermediate Acoustic Blues Guitar* and *Mastering Acoustic Blues Guitar*.) Track 1 for each book will help you tune your guitar.

See page 1 for instructions on how to access the online audio.

CHAPTER 1

Review: Learning the Fretboard

INTERVALS AND SCALES

Remember, an *interval* is the distance in pitch between two notes. Two intervals you should be very familiar with are the *half step* (the distance of one fret) and the *whole step* (the distance of two frets). An *octave* is the distance of 12 half steps between two notes with the same name. A *scale* is a series of tones arranged in a particular pattern of half steps and whole steps.

CHROMATIC SCALE

An understanding of the *chromatic scale* will help you to name the notes on the fretboard. The chromatic scale is a scale consisting of all 12 half steps in an octave. So it is made up of all the *natural* notes (A–B–C–D–E–F–G) and all the notes in between (the *altered* notes, see below). The illustration below starts and ends with C, but the chromatic scale can start on any note. The white keys on the keyboard are the natural notes and the black keys are the *altered* notes. These are notes modified by a *sharp* (which raises the pitch of a note by a half step) or *flat* (which lowers the pitch of a note by a half step).

The Chromatic Scale on the Keyboard

Notice there are no sharps or flats between E and F and B and C. Notice also that the black keys have two names (for example: C♯/D♭, D♯/E♭, etc.). These are *enharmonic equivalents,* which are two notes that have the same pitch (sound exactly the same) but are spelled differently.

On the guitar we do not have the visual aid of black and white keys—all the frets look the same. However, the same chromatic or half-step principle makes it easy for us to name every note on the guitar. The following illustration gives the names of the pitches on each string—from the open string to the 17th fret.

Fretboard Diagram

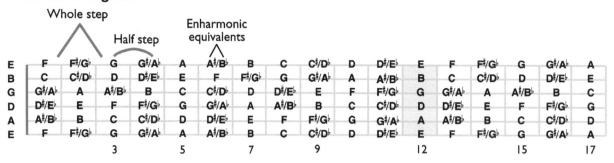

If you start with any open string and go 12 half steps (12 frets) up (toward the body), you will have gone the distance of an octave and played every pitch-name there is. Notice also, you will have arrived at the letter with which you started. E is the open 1st string; if you go to the 12th fret, you arrive again at E. This is the same for all the strings and for every pitch.

Learning the fretboard is essential. You can do this by first memorizing the natural notes on each string. Once you have these down, you can then locate the sharps and flats in relation to the natural notes.

Dave Van Ronk (1936–2002) was a folk singer and guitarist who played a major role in the folk revival of the 1960s. In addition to his own achievements as a musician, he lent a helping hand to many up-and-coming artists of the time, like Bob Dylan and Joni Mitchell.

TRANSPOSING

If you can locate the notes on the fretboard, you will be able to *transpose* or move the chords, scales, phrases and songs in this book to new positions and *keys* (a key is the set of all notes belonging to a particular scale). Two reasons why you may choose to do this are: 1) To accommodate the pitch range of a singer you are accompanying, 2) You prefer the sound of the tune in a higher or lower key.

For an example of transposition, check out the E7#9 chord below.

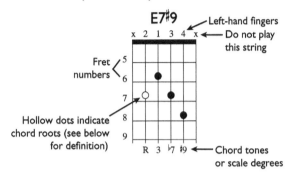

This is a popular chord in funk, blues and rock 'n' roll. It's often played as illustrated above—in E. However, you should be able to move anything you play to other keys. Let's move this 7#9 chord to G.

Notice that the *root* (the note on which the chord is built, also known as "1") is on the 5th string. So to play a G7#9 you'll need to find a G on the 5th string. The open 5th string is an A and the fretted notes on the string progress upward through the chromatic scale. So start by counting up from A#/B♭ on the 1st fret, to B on the 2nd, C on the 3rd, etc. Do this until you reach the G on the 10th fret. Now use the fingering for the E7#9 above, but place its root on the G on the 10th fret of the 5th string—and you have a G7#9. Check it out below.

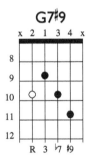

Now that you've seen how to move a chord to a new letter name on the neck you should be able to do this with any other chord, scale, phrase or song. To become a blues master you must be able to transpose *all* the music you learn to any key. This process will help prepare you for any musical situation.

CHAPTER 2

Fingerstyle in A

This chapter demonstrates a few approaches to blues fingerstyle in the key of A (made up of all the notes of the A Major scale). "12 to the Bar" consists of moving *6ths* (intervals that are six scale degrees apart) with a *monotonic bass* pattern. A monotonic bass consists of repeated root notes played on the lower (4th, 5th and 6th) strings with the thumb. Although this piece has a *melody* or tune, it would make a great accompaniment to a blues vocal. See the list to the right for abbreviations for the right-hand fingers.

Right-Hand Fingers
- *pulgar (p)* for thumb
- *indice (i)* for index
- *medio (m)* for middle
- *anular (a)* for ring

12 TO THE BAR

Track 2

This next piece moves our 6ths to the upper strings for an even more melodic sound. "Sixthsville" is played with a *swing* rhythm (indicated by the caption: *Swing 8ths*). In this type of rhythm, two eighth notes are played like a *triplet*—three notes played in the time of two—with the first two eighth notes tied together ♪♪ = ♪♪). Also, watch the *slides, hammer-ons* and *pull-offs*. These are basic left-hand techniques explained in-depth in the first two books of this series.

SL ⟋ = Ascending slide

SL ⟍ = Descending slide

H = Hammer-on

P = Pull-off

SIXTHSVILLE

Track 3

The next song is dedicated to John Jackson, a great player and person who shared his music with countless students at the National Guitar Workshop. In this tune, the timing for the slides and hammer-ons is tricky (for example: the second *double stop*—two notes played at the same time—of the first slide is above a picked bass note). Practice these parts slowly at first, as many times as it takes, and be sure to use the recording as a guide.

SWINGIN' AWAY IN A

Track 4

CHAPTER 3

Fingerstyle in C, Amin and G

Reverend Gary Davis was one of the most popular performers in the country blues revival of the 1960s. He was a teacher to some of the most important young players who carried on the acoustic blues torch. Dave Van Ronk, Stefan Grossman, Roy Book Binder and Ian Buchanan all took lessons with him and countless others were influenced by his exciting approach to blues and gospel guitar. This piece is based on his style of blending *alternating bass* patterns (where the bass notes of the chords alternate between two or more notes on the lower strings) with fast single-note runs. This is in the key of C.

≀ = Strum with finger.

T = Left-hand thumb in fingering below the TAB

ROCKIN' WITH THE REVEREND

Track 5

This bluesy piece is in the key of A Minor and is based on a repeated Amin–F7–E7 *progression* (series of chords). Progressions like this are found in traditional Dixieland jazz style and were imitated by blues players. At first, the Amin is played in *1st position* (which means the 1st finger is located at the 1st fret). Later in the tune, however, it is moved up the neck to the 5th position (1st finger located at the 5th fret). This piece features a lot of *syncopated* rhythms, with chords being played on *upbeats* (last beat of a measure) before the *downbeats* (first beat of a measure). In general, syncopation shifts the emphasis from the *onbeats* where you would tap your foot *down* (1, 2, 3, 4) to the *offbeats* where you bring your foot *up* (the "&s"). This gives the piece a feeling of forward momentum and drive.

WHITE HOLLOW BLUES

Track 6

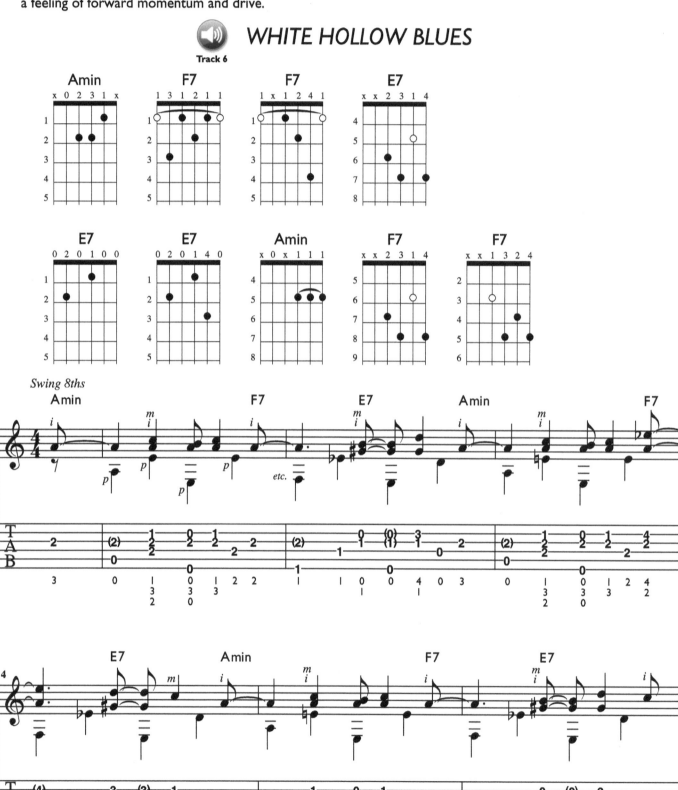

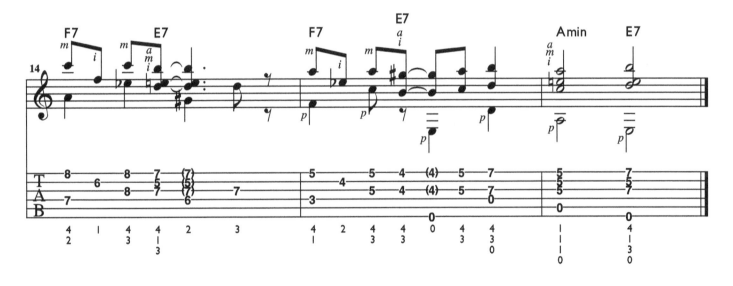

The next piece is in the key of G, in which all Fs are sharp. The steady beat, the alternating bass (G–D–G–E) and the syncopated licks on the upper strings are all in the style of the great Mississippi John Hurt.

MISSISSIPPI MAN

Track 7

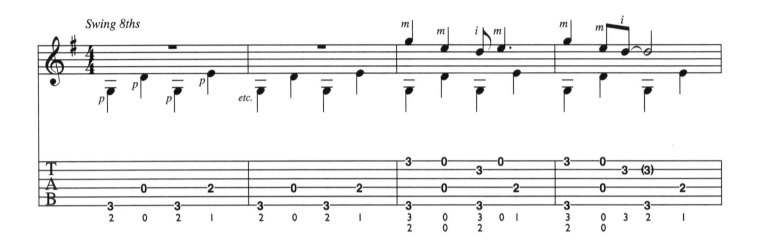

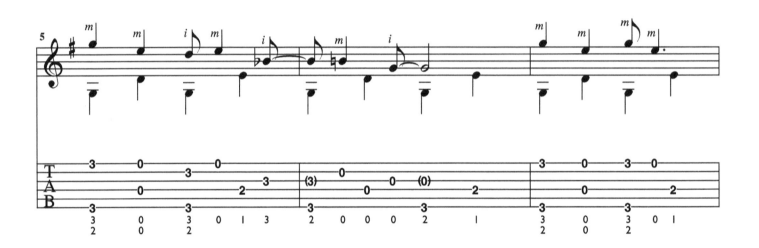

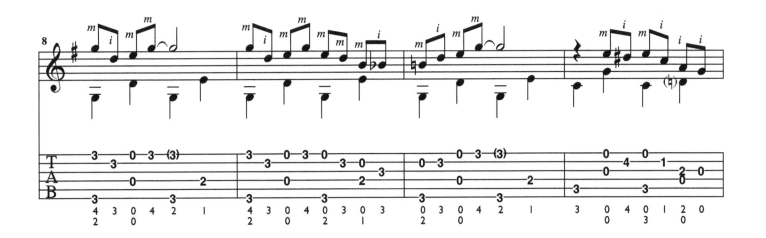

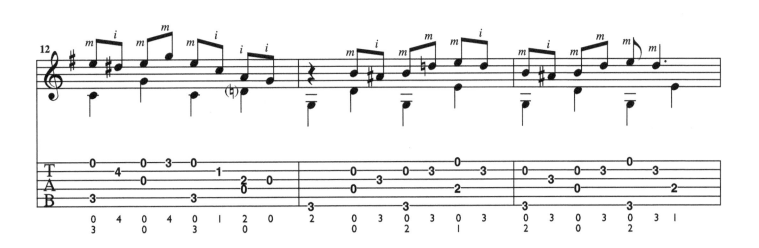

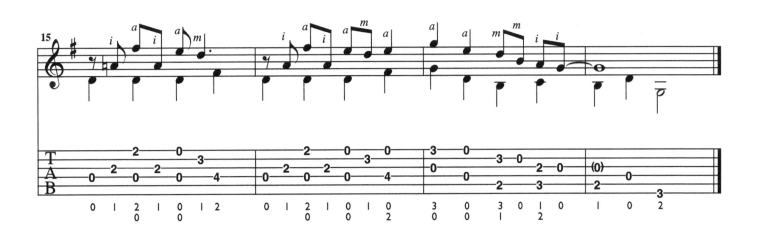

CHAPTER 4

Minor Pentatonic Scale

The *minor pentatonic scale* is a five-note scale and is one of the most often played scales in the blues (and many other styles as well). The average player working through this book is probably already well-acquainted with this scale. Form 1 of this scale (see page 186) is often the first scale guitarists learn. However, players are not always familiar with many variations of this important scale.

Learning the five fingerings in this book—and how to connect them—will allow you to move up and down the neck as you improvise. Instead of being stuck in one position, you will be able to glide from one position to another and take your phrases higher or lower as you hear them in your mind. Your playing will improve and you'll feel more confident because of your ability to play up and down the fretboard with no gaps. This won't happen overnight, but it will happen eventually if you keep at it. Practice improvising with each new fingering, and work on connecting each fingering to the next one in the series.

First we'll spend a little time on the theory behind the minor pentatonic scale. Then we'll get into the fingerings. For a more in-depth look at blues theory take a look at the *Beginning* and *Intermediate* books in this series.

MINOR PENTATONIC SCALE THEORY

We can use the *major scale* as a guide to help us understand other scales and chords. The major scale consists of seven notes and is arranged in this order of whole steps (W) and half steps (H): W–W–H–W–W–W–H. Each note in a scale is a *scale degree* and is numbered consecutively from 1 (the tonic) to 7.

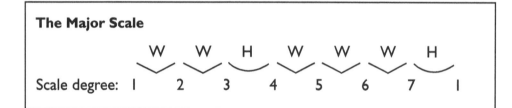

Here are the notes in a G Major scale:

= Downstroke

Now let's look at the G Minor Pentatonic scale as it relates to the above G Major scale.

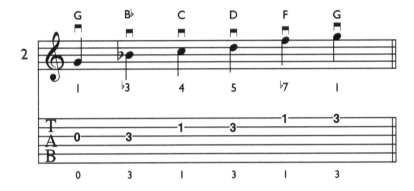

The minor pentatonic scale consists of scale degrees: 1–$\flat$3–4–5–$\flat$7. For a sense of completion, we end on the 1 (G) in a higher octave. If we compare the major scale and minor pentatonic scale, we see that the minor pentatonic has the same 1, 4 and 5 as the major scale. It does not have a 3 or 7, but *does* have a $\flat$3 and $\flat$7. To *flat* a note we lower it one half step, so the $\flat$3 is B$\flat$—one half step lower than B. The 7 in the G Major scale, F$\sharp$, is flatted to an F$\natural$. The 2 and 6 of the major scale are totally omitted from the minor pentatonic scale.

Whatever note we start on, every minor pentatonic scale consists of: 1–$\flat$3–4–5–$\flat$7. This is the magic formula. The $\flat$3 and $\flat$7 are *blue notes* and are vital to the sound of the blues.

Below is the most common form of the minor pentatonic scale. It is often the first scale learned by beginning guitar players. We'll play it in the key of G, starting in the 3rd position. This will leave plenty of room on the fretboard to play the other four forms.

G Minor Pentatonic Scale—Form I

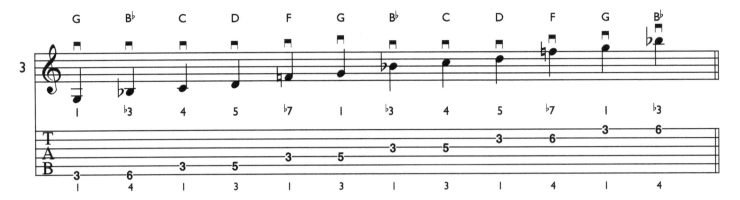

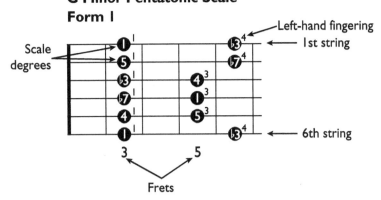

G Minor Pentatonic Scale
Form I

On page 187 are some cool blues phrases based on this great scale form. Memorize and use them in your own solos. Note that they use *pull-offs* and *bends*—two cool left-hand techniques covered in detail in the previous two books.

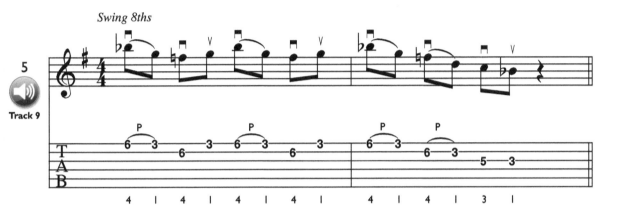

For a *quarter-step bend*, bend to the pitch halfway to the next fret. This produces a real bluesy sound.

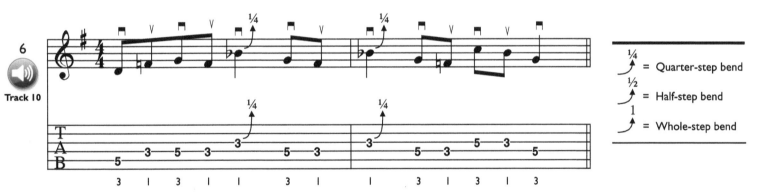

Form 2 of the minor pentatonic scale has the same notes (G–B♭–C–D–F) as Form 1, but they lie in a different pattern. Each of our five fingerings will have the same five notes, but in different patterns and octaves. You may ask, "Why learn five fingerings if they all have the same notes?" Because each new form takes us a little higher up the neck, and its unique pattern gives us new phrasing possibilities and ideas.

Notice that Form 2 has slightly different fingerings when ascending and descending. This is because there is a one-fret *shift* (change of position) that occurs when we reach the 2nd string. This shift allows us to use our 1st and 3rd fingers on the 1st and 2nd strings. These strong fingers will help us to execute bends, hammer-ons, pull-offs and other left-hand techniques on these often played strings.

G Minor Pentatonic Scale—Form 2

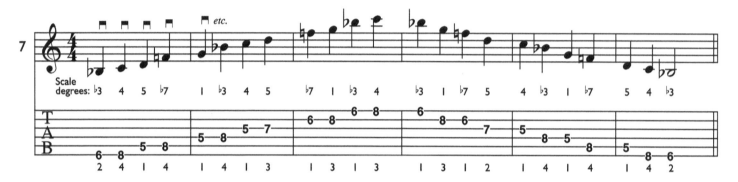

G Minor Pentatonic Scale Form 2—Ascending

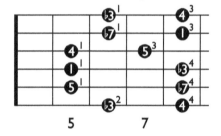

G Minor Pentatonic Scale Form 2—Descending

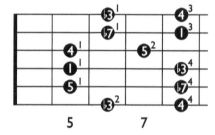

The following phrases are based on Form 2 of the minor pentatonic scale. The first example has a *whole-step bend* on the first beat of the second measure. This is a left-hand technique where you bend a note to the pitch of a note a whole step higher. Notice that the first note in the bend is a *grace note* ♪. This is a small note played quickly before the *destination note* to which you are bending.

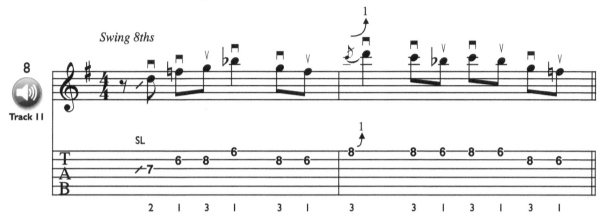

This example features *vibrato* on the last note. Vibrato is a series of quick, tiny bends that create a cool, twangy sound. Vibrato is a trademark of such blues greats as B. B. King.

〰 = Vibrato

This next example has hammer-ons, slides and vibrato. You will be playing double stops and hammering-on to a second note while keeping both strings ringing.

CONNECTING FORMS 1 AND 2

Now that we have looked at the first two minor pentatonic fingerings separately, we can look at how they connect to each other.

Look at each string in Form 1 and compare it to the same string in Form 2. Notice that the *highest* note on each string in Form 1 is the same note as the *lowest* note on each string in Form 2. For example, on the 6th string in Form 1, we go from the 1 to the ♭3. On the 6th string in Form 2 we go from the *same* ♭3 to the 4. This is how our two forms connect. You'll soon see that all of the other minor pentatonic scale fingerings connect in the same manner.

G Minor Pentatonic Scale Form 1

G Minor Pentatonic Scale Form 2

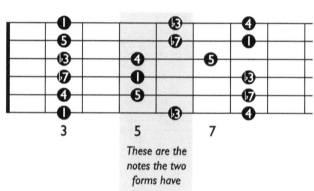

The illustration to the right shows how the two fingerings look when they are connected on the fretboard.

The example below illustrates how we can move from Form 1 to Form 2 with a shift on the 1st string. When you have this down, learn to shift fingerings on *each* of the other strings. Do this with *all* the minor pentatonic scale forms in this book and you'll be comfortable shifting positions up and down the fretboard as you improvise solos.

Forms 1 and 2 Connected

These are the notes the two forms have in common

In the following two examples, we move between forms with a shift on the 3rd string. This is a common string on which to shift, but make up your own phrases and try shifting on other strings as well.

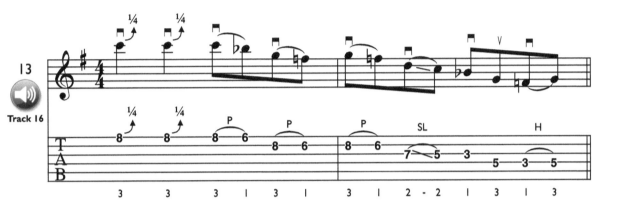

It's time to do some improvising! Below is a progression for a G Blues. Play along to the backing track on the recording. Improvise using the scale forms and sample licks you've learned so far.

 BLUES BACKING TRACK

Track 17

CHAPTER 5

Fingerstyle in E

As you probably know, the key of E (which has four sharps) is one of the most popular keys for the blues. The pieces in this section contain many of the classic phrases that are found in the blues repertoire.

Big Bill Broonzy was one of the most influential acoustic blues players. He was popular in the U.S. and also toured England, where he had an impact on many of the guitarists who were involved in the British blues movement of the early '60s.

BIG BILL'S BLUES

Track 18

In this piece, there are several slides up to the E on the 5th string, 7th fret. Start from the B on the 2nd fret and slide to the E as fast as you can. Big Bill Broonzy used this sliding technique in some of his music.

UP THE FIFTH

Track 19

"Leaving Chicago" mixes the world's most popular *shuffle* style blues riffs on the lower three strings with short, melodic phrases on the upper three. Shuffle style is characterized by the repetitive rhythmic figure of quarter note followed by an eighth note in $\frac{12}{8}$ time. If you find this tune rhythmically difficult, review it one bar at a time. It starts with a great *turnaround* intro in the style of Robert Johnson and many other country blues greats. A turnaround is usually found in the last two bars of a tune and sets the music up to either repeat the form or end.

LEAVING CHICAGO

Track 20

CHAPTER 6

More Minor Pentatonic Scale Forms

For our third and fourth forms of the minor pentatonic scale, we'll stay in the key of G (like we did for Forms 1 and 2). This will help us see how they fit together in sequence on the fretboard. Once you can move between them all in G, you can start practicing them in other keys.

MINOR PENTATONIC SCALE—FORM 3

G Minor Pentatonic Scale—Form 3

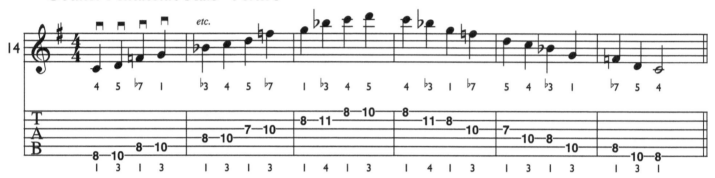

**G Minor Pentatonic Scale
Form 3**

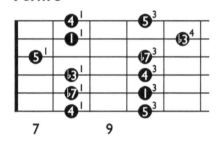

Check out the following two phrases based on Form 3. They include hammer-ons on the 5th and 6th strings. Hammer-ons and pull-offs are easy to play on these strings because of their uniform whole-step pattern. Note the dots above the F♯ and D in the first measure. They signify *staccato*, which tells you to play the notes in a short, detached fashion.

◉ = *Staccato.* Play in a short, detached fashion.

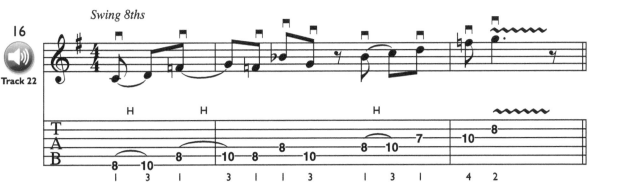

CONNECTING FORMS 2 AND 3

When you are comfortable with Form 3, work on connecting it with Form 2. Here is how they look together.

Forms 2 and 3 Connected

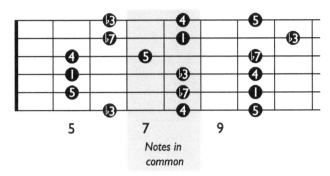

The exercise below shifts from Form 2 to 3 on the 2nd string, then moves back to Form 2 on the 4th string. Be sure to practice shifting on other strings as well.

Forms 2 and 3 are combined in the example below. Note that each three-note grouping consists of a hammer-on followed by a pull-off. For these you pick only the first note of the group. If you cannot play these smoothly at first, be sure to practice them separately.

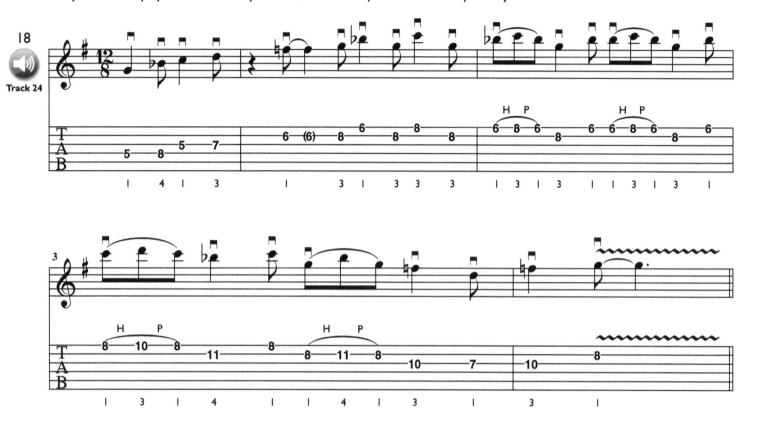

MINOR PENTATONIC SCALE—FORM 4

After Form 1, Form 4 is perhaps the easiest to memorize and play because you stay in one position.

G Minor Pentatonic Scale—Form 4

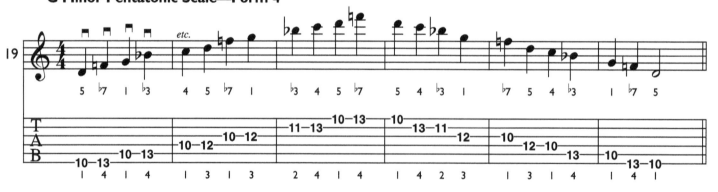

G Minor Pentatonic Scale
Form 4

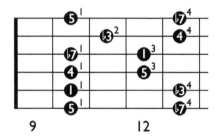

One way to create your own phrases is to modify others that you learn. You can change the rhythm or the direction of the notes, or just repeat certain parts. Use this approach with the following examples. They are based on Form 4 of the minor pentatonic scale.

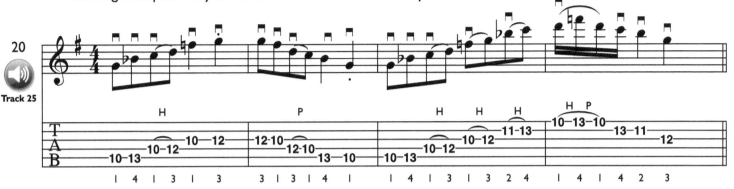

This next phrase starts with a C that is bent up to the pitch of D. This bent note is held and keeps ringing as the next note, F, is picked. The F should continue to ring as the bent note is brought down to its original sound of C in a *reverse bend*. Note that we are using the 3rd finger to fret the first note of the bend. This makes the bend easier and more effective.

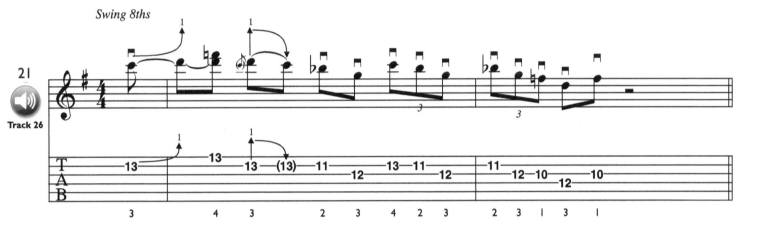

When you feel comfortable with Form 4, learn to connect it to Form 3 by shifting on each string. Here's what they look like together.

Forms 3 and 4 Connected

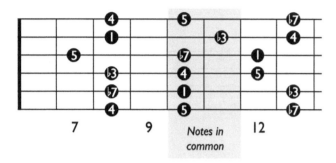

This exercise connects Forms 3 and 4 by shifting positions on the 2nd string.

These phrases move between Forms 3 and 4. In the first example, the C that is bent to D on the 2nd string should be held to blend with the next note, D, that is played on the 1st string.

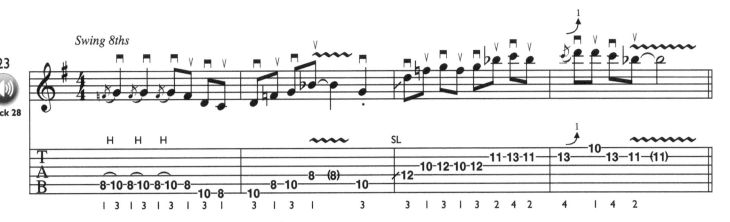

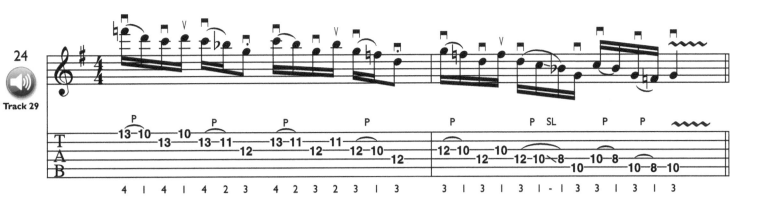

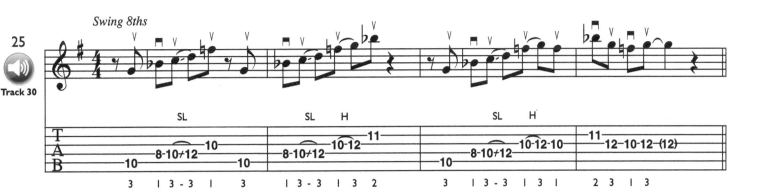

CHAPTER 7

Fingerstyle in Drop D

Drop D is an *altered tuning*. An altered tuning is any tuning *other* than *standard tuning*: E–A–D–G–B–E. To tune your guitar to drop D, all you need to do is tune the 6th string down a whole step from E to D. In this tuning, any song in the key of D will have a richer and stronger sound. It is a great tuning that's been used by Tommy Johnson, Bonnie Raitt, Blind Willie McTell and almost anyone who ever played in the key of D.

"The Lowdown D Blues" has a steady alternating bass that gives the piece a strong sound. It also has some chord shapes that may be new to you; practice them separately until you can grab them with ease.

THE LOWDOWN D BLUES

This next piece contains some of the most popular fingerstyle blues riffs for the key of D. It's in the style of Blind Willie McTell.

WILLIE WAS HERE

Track 32

CHAPTER 8

Another Minor Pentatonic Scale Form

MINOR PENTATONIC SCALE—FORM 5

Our fifth and last minor pentatonic scale fingering will once again be in the key of G. In G, this fingering is in the 12th position. This may make it a bit more difficult to play, but you should be able to reach its highest notes on the 15th fret with a little practice. Of course, if your guitar has a cutaway, you're all set.

G Minor Pentatonic Scale—Form 5

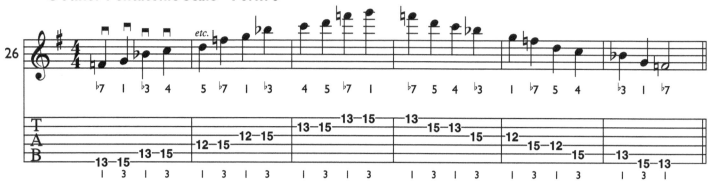

G Minor Pentatonic Scale
Form 5

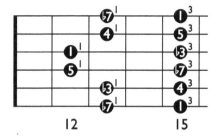

The pattern on the first two strings in Form 5 makes hammer-ons and pull-offs natural phrasing choices. Check this out.

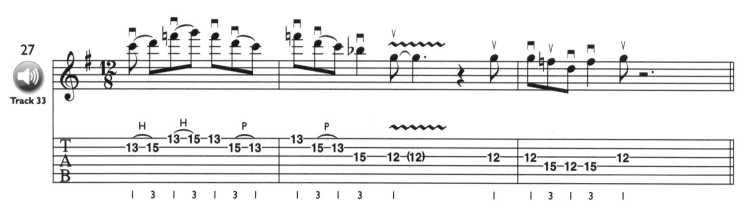

Track 33

Connecting Forms 4 and 5 in the key of G brings us higher up the fretboard. This is a popular area for improvisers.

Forms 4 and 5 Connected

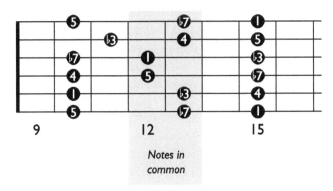

This exercise shifts from Form 4 to 5 on the 4th string and then back to Form 4 on the 3rd string.

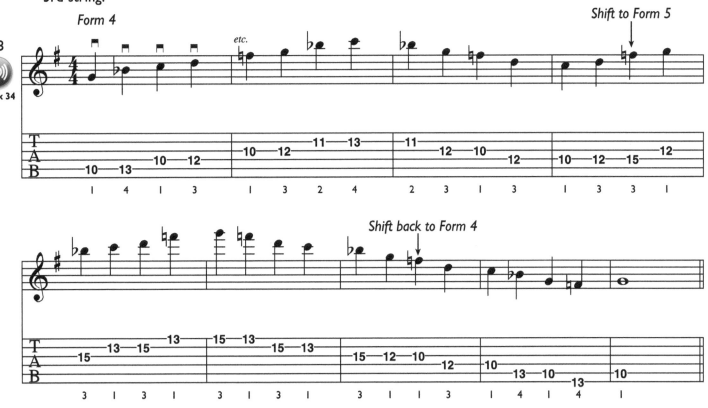

This example in $\frac{12}{8}$ starts in Form 5 then shifts down to Form 4.

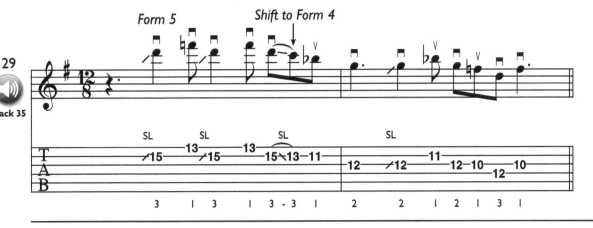

CHAPTER 9

Open Tunings

Delta bluesmen like Charley Patton, Son House and Robert Johnson made extensive use of *open G* and *open D tunings.* East coast players also used them in their music. In an open tuning, all the strings are tuned to the notes of a major or minor chord. In *open A,* the strings have the same relationships as in open G, they are all just a whole step higher. In *open E,* the strings have the same relationships, but are all a whole step higher than open D. Though open A and E are brighter sounding—and are sometimes used for slide playing—the lower tunings will give you a deeper blues sound.

OPEN D TUNING

To tune to open D, lower the 1st and 6th strings a whole step to D; lower the 2nd string a whole step to A; and lower the 3rd string a half step to F♯. From the 6th string to the 1st, your strings should be tuned: D–A–D–F♯–A–D. "Down Deep in D" is in open D and contains some phrases and positions used often in this tuning.

DOWN DEEP IN D

In open G tuning, the strings (from 6th to 1st) are tuned: D–G–D–G–B–D. All you need to do is tune down the 1st, 5th and 6th strings a whole step—the 1st and 6th from E to D, and the 5th from A to G. "Blues for Skip" is dedicated to Skip James. He played in open G and other alternate tunings and created a distinctive sound through his unusual rhythmic approach and unique falsetto* vocals. Note the change of time signature to $\frac{6}{8}$ in measure 5 and back to $\frac{12}{8}$ in measure 6.

BLUES FOR SKIP

Track 37

Open G Tuning

* Vocal technique used to extend the voice beyond its "normal" range.

The piece below has a steady alternating bass pattern and some real bluesy sounding bends. Also, in bar 11, you'll hit a chord shape that looks like a C in standard tuning, but it's a C7 in open G tuning (see chord diagram to the right). This funky chord with its $\flat$7 in the bass was used by Mississippi Fred McDowell and many others.

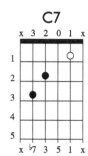

 KEEP IT STEADY FREDDIE

Track 38

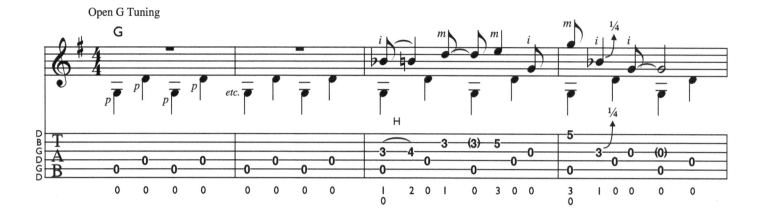

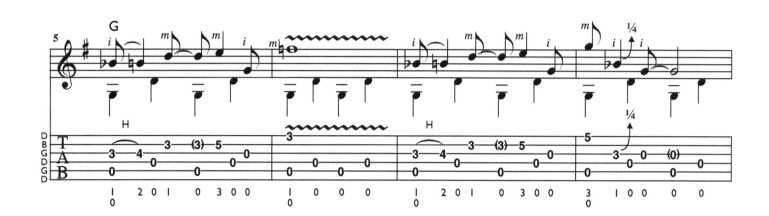

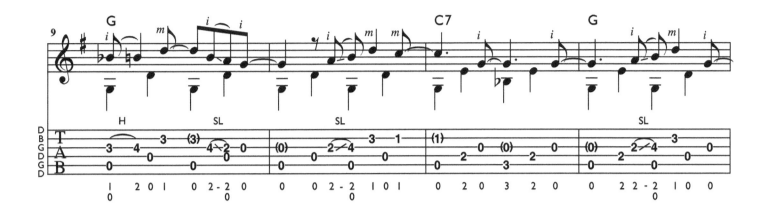

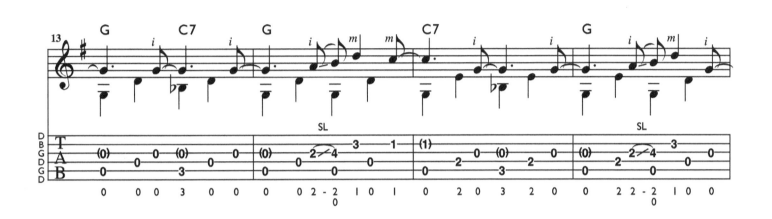

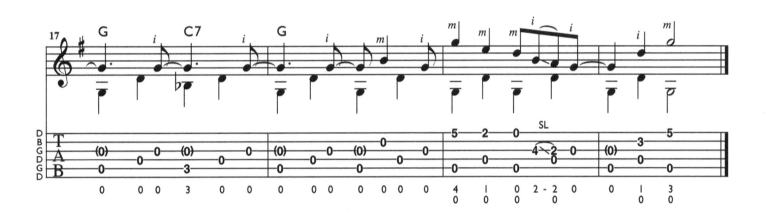

CHAPTER 10

Major Pentatonic Scale

In this chapter, we'll take an in-depth look at the *major pentatonic scale*. You learned one fingering for the scale in the first two books in this series, but a "blues master" needs to know all five. This scale consists of scale degrees: 1–2–3–5–6. It's often used over the I chord in a key (see below). It can also be used over the IV chord if you change the tonic of the scale to match the root of the chord. For example: In the key of C, the IV chord is an F, so use an F Major Pentatonic scale.

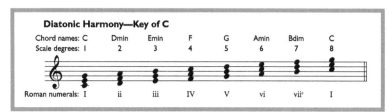

G Major Pentatonic Scale
Form 1

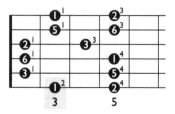

As you learn these five versions of the major pentatonic scale, notice they have the same fingering patterns as the five minor pentatonic scales. Form 1 of the major pentatonic scale has the same pattern as Form 2 of the minor pentatonic scale (see diagrams to the right); Form 2 of the major pentatonic scale has the same pattern as Form 3 of the minor pentatonic scale, etc. Form 5 of the major pentatonic scale has the same pattern as Form 1 of the minor pentatonic scale. Although the fingering patterns for the major pentatonic and minor pentatonic scales are related in this way, the notes are different. For instance, in the diagram of the G Major Pentatonic scale to the right, the first note on the 6th string is a 1 (G). However, the correlating note on the G Minor Pentatonic scale (also to the right) is $\flat$3 (B$\flat$).

G Minor Pentatonic Scale
Form 2

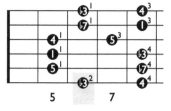

Let's take a quick look at *why* the minor and major pentatonic scales share fingering patterns. Below are the G Major and G Major Pentatonic scales. You can see that the 1, 2, 3, 5 and 6 of the major scale make up the major pentatonic scale and give us the notes: G–A–B–D–E.

G Major Scale

G Major Pentatonic Scale

Now look at the E Major and E Minor Pentatonic scales below.

E Major Scale

E Minor Pentatonic Scale

The minor pentatonic scale consists of scale degrees: 1–♭3–4–5–♭7. In the key of E Minor, the notes are: E–G–A–B–D. Although they have different tonics and scale degrees, the E Minor and G Major Pentatonic scales share exactly the same notes.

	6	1	2	3	5	6
G Major Pentatonic Scale:	(E) –	G –	A –	B –	D –	E
	1	♭3	4	5	♭7	1
E Minor Pentatonic Scale:	E –	G –	A –	B –	D –	(E)

This will make it easy for you to memorize the major pentatonic fingerings, but be sure to learn the locations of all the tonics—they are good starting, ending and *target notes* (notes around which your licks and phrases revolve) for your solos. Also learn the locations of the 3s and 5s; they are great target notes as well.

As you make your way through the major pentatonic scale forms, be sure to memorize each scale and come up with your own licks and phrases for each one. Then practice shifting from one to another like we did with the minor pentatonic scale forms.

MAJOR PENTATONIC SCALE—FORM 1

G Major Pentatonic Scale—Form 1

G Major Pentatonic Scale
Form 1—Ascending

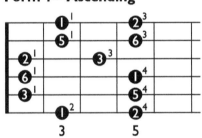

G Major Pentatonic Scale
Form 1—Descending

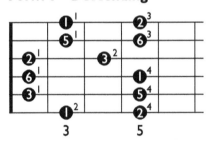

Here's an example using Form 1 of the G Major Pentatonic scale.

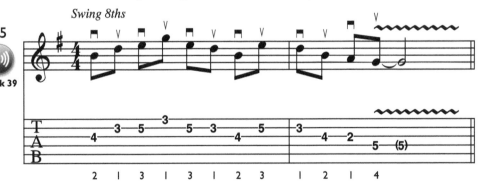

NOTE: All the fingerings and phrases in this chapter are in the key of G to enable you to see the relationships between them. When you're comfortable with them in the key of G, transpose them to other common blues keys.

G Major Pentatonic Scale—Form 2

**G Major Pentatonic Scale
Form 2**

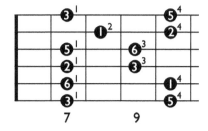

G Major Pentatonic Scale—Form 3

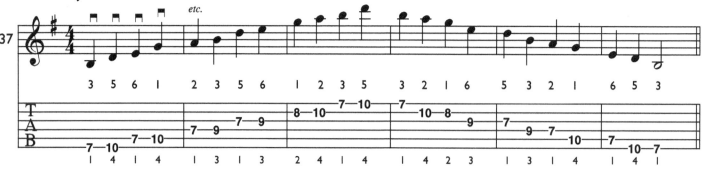

**G Major Pentatonic Scale
Form 3**

This is an example using the Form 3 fingering.

Track 40

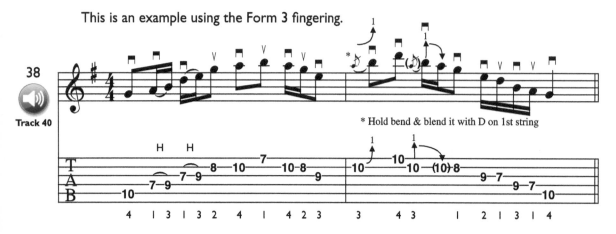

* Hold bend & blend it with D on 1st string

G Major Pentatonic Scale—Form 4

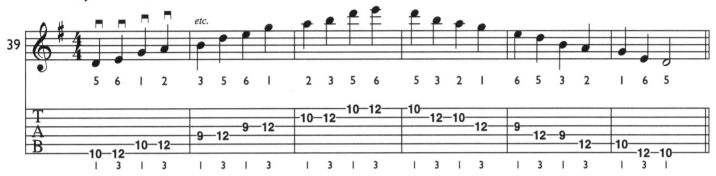

G Major Pentatonic Scale
Form 4

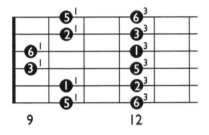

G Major Pentatonic Scale—Form 5

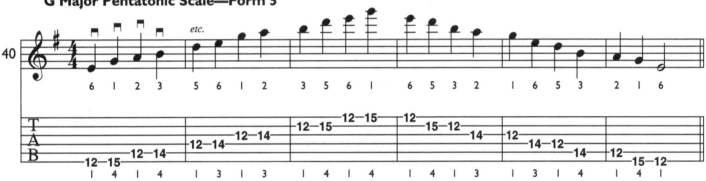

G Major Pentatonic Scale
Form 5

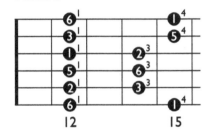

This example demonstrates ways to shift smoothly between Forms 1–4.

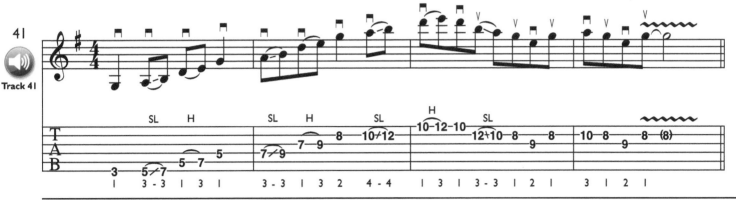

CHAPTER 11

Slide in Standard Tuning

What is the sound of blues guitar? Of course, there are a multitude of *timbres* (tone qualities; pronounced TAM-bers) and styles that are found under the umbrella of the blues, but many would say that no sound epitomizes the feeling of the blues as well as slide guitar.

A *slide* is a plastic, metal or glass cylinder, open on both ends, that you place on your left-hand pinky or ring finger.

Plastic, glass and metal slides.

You use this to slide from note to note or chord to chord, producing a very fluid and smooth sound that is often used to imitate the human voice. You can play slide on almost any steel-string guitar, but this style works best on an instrument with high *action*. The term, action, refers to how high or low the strings are above the fretboard. Normally, it is not desirable to have the strings too high because this makes them hard to press. However, not much fretting takes place in slide style and higher action allows the slide to glide along the strings without scraping the fretboard or frets. Higher strings will give you a cleaner sound.

Thicker strings are also an advantage in slide playing. They will give you a stronger tone and more resistance, so it will be easier to keep the slide from hitting the neck. If you regularly use light gauge strings you may want to move up to medium; some players will even use heavy gauge strings.

If you are going to be doing a lot of slide playing, you may want to consider getting a separate guitar. You can have a repair person raise the action and make adjustments to accommodate heavier gauge strings.

Slide Guitar Tips

- **Wear the slide on your pinky.** This leaves three fingers free for playing chords and phrases without the slide.

- **Move the slide along the strings very lightly.** The slide should glide along the string and not press down into it. It should never touch the fretboard; any depression of the string should be minimal.

- **When playing chords with the slide, keep it perpendicular to the frets.** If it's on an angle, the notes in the chord will sound out of tune.

- **When playing on the 1st string, angle the slide to touch this string while missing all the others.** This will help you achieve a clean sound. A lot of slide playing occurs on this string for that reason.

- **Make sure to place the slide directly over the fret wire** (see picture below). This is the only way a note will sound in tune. Good intonation is one of the challenges of slide playing. Vibrato is a colorful technique slide players use to help them play in tune.

Place the slide directly over the fret wire.

- **Use vibrato.** This is the wavering effect most often used on longer notes and final notes in phrases. To apply vibrato with a slide, move the slide quickly back and forth over a note or chord. Try this with various notes until your vibrato is smooth. Since the frets get smaller as they go up the neck, you will have to adapt your motion to whatever fret you are at. The speed of your vibrato can be faster or slower depending upon your style and the sound you are trying to achieve. Listen to the great slide players and soak up their influence. Robert Johnson, Blind Willie Johnson and Ry Cooder should be on any acoustic slide players listening list. Also, be sure to listen to the examples on the recording.

- **Slide players generally do not play with picks.** Instead, they use a fingerstyle approach. Even if you normally use a pick, you should try playing fingerstyle when playing slide guitar. You'll get a great tone and will be in a better position for right-hand muting. Use your thumb to pick notes on the lower stings and your other fingers to play the upper ones. It's common to rely on the 1st and 2nd fingers much more than the 3rd or ring finger.

- **Mute unwanted sounds with your right hand.** A slide will naturally produce unwanted sounds when moving along the strings. You'll play a note on one string but the slide will touch and sound other strings as well. Also, the string length behind the slide (the length from the slide to the nut) will invariably vibrate and produce sounds. This makes it difficult to get a clean and clear sound and makes muting technique vital to good slide playing. This involves picking a string with one finger while resting any unused fingers on the strings that are not being picked. For example, when picking the 2nd string with the middle finger *(m)*, your ring finger *(a)* can touch and mute the 1st string. The index finger *(i)* can mute the 3rd string, and your thumb *(p)* can rest lightly over the lower three strings. This may take a while to get used to, but it will reduce unwanted noises and will give you a cleaner sound.

- **Mute unwanted sounds with your left hand.** When sliding to a note, let your left hand fingers (especially the first)—that are behind the slide—lightly drag along the strings. This will stop them from vibrating and reduce unwanted noise.

NOTE: The notation for slide technique is the same as when sliding without a slide on your finger. An "s" in the left-hand fingering under the TAB indicates notes or chords played by the slide.

The following examples demonstrate some typical slide moves using the open strings. Be sure to mute the strings you're not playing. Listen for any unwanted buzzing sounds. Also, be sure to get that rapid vibrato on the quarter notes.

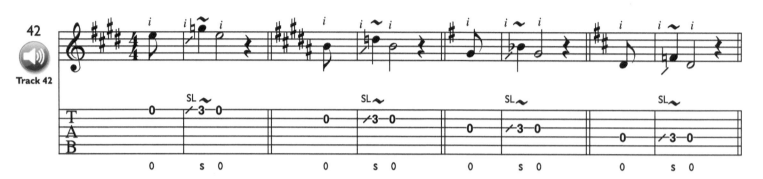

Here are some more slide examples. You can try these and the licks in Example 42 on the 5th and 6ths strings as well.

Here's a cool slide lick played on the top four strings.

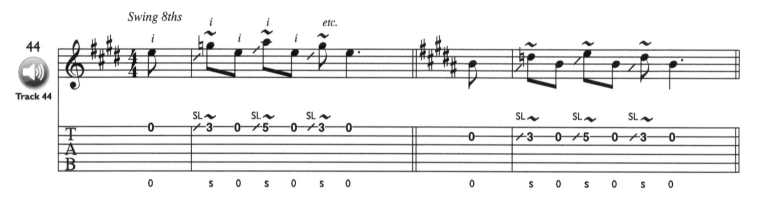

A lot of slide work takes place on one string. It's nice to know that even if you break five strings at a gig, you can still play something cool. Here are two more single-string phrases to check out. The first is in the key of E on the 1st string. The second is in G and contains the complete G Minor Pentatonic scale.

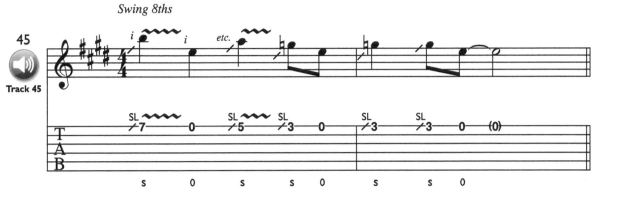

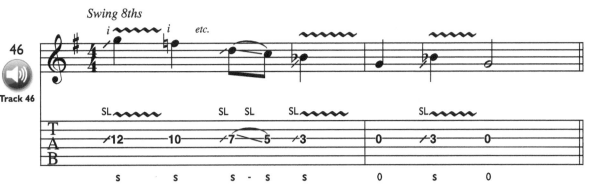

Here are a couple popular slide licks in the key of E.

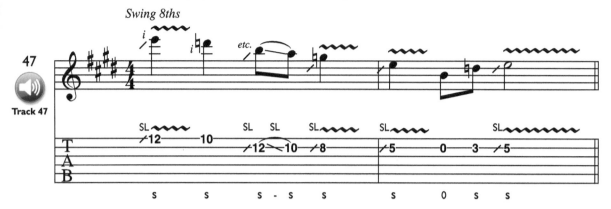

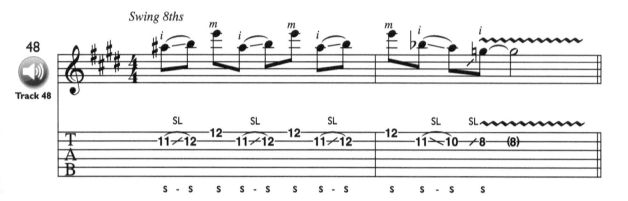

The next example is in the key of G and is based on the G chord (G–B–D) that is formed on the 12 fret of the 2nd, 3rd and 4th strings. There are double-stop slides and slides to the chord tones. You cannot easily transfer this phrase to other sets of strings, but you can transpose the G chord (and its accompanying licks) by moving it to other frets. For example: In the key of G, the IV chord, C, would be on the 5th fret, and the V chord, D, would be on the 7th.

Slide players love to hit a low note and play licks and phrases above it. The following piece in
E demonstrates this cool way of playing. Listen to the recording to get a feel for it. The low Es
that start each bar are played staccato. After you strike them with your thumb, mute them by
touching the 6th string with the fleshy part of your hand, where your thumb joins your palm.

HIT THE SIX

Track 50

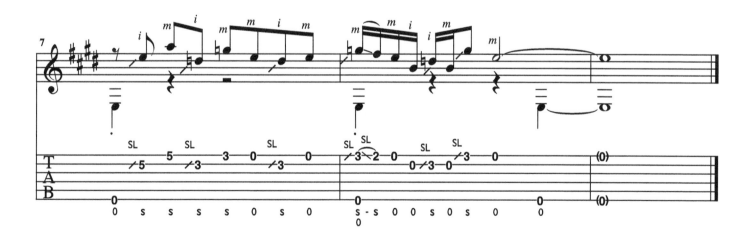

For more great slide tunes, see Chapter 16 (page 230).

CHAPTER 12

Blues Scale

The *blues scale* consists of scale degrees: 1–♭3–4–♭5–5–♭7. It is identical to the minor pentatonic scale with the addition of the ♭5 or its enharmonic equivalent, a ♯4. Whether written as a ♯4 or a ♭5, in this book we will refer to this unique sound as ♭5 for the sake of convenience. So, if you have all the minor pentatonic fingerings down, learning the five blues scale fingerings should not be too challenging. This chapter introduces all five forms of the blues scale. Memorize and use them to improvise solos. Targeting the ♭5s will bring out the color of this great scale. All our examples are in the key of G. When you're comfortable with this key, be sure to transpose them to other keys.

BLUES SCALE—FORM 1

G Blues Scale—Form 1

G Blues Scale
Form 1

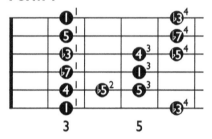

BLUES SCALE—FORM 2

G Blues Scale—Form 2

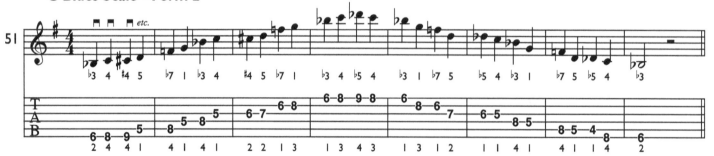

G Blues Scale
Form 2—Ascending

G Blues Scale
Form 2—Descending

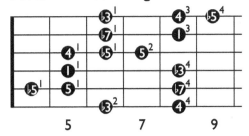

This example is based on Forms 1 and 2.

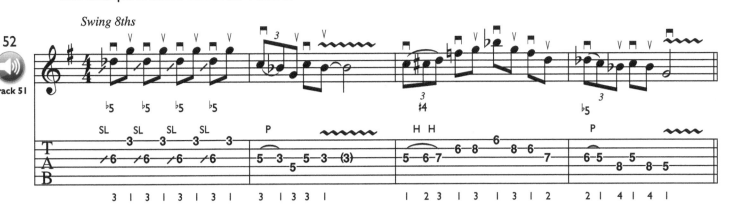

BLUES SCALE—FORM 3

G Blues Scale—Form 3

G Blues Scale
Form 3

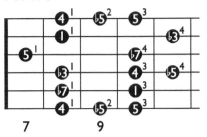

G Blues Scale—Form 4

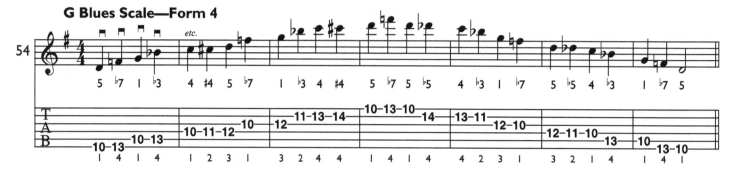

G Blues Scale
Form 4

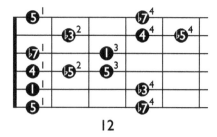

12

This lick is based on Forms 3 and 4 of the blues scale.

Track 52

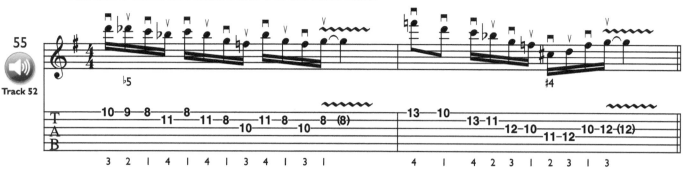

G Blues Scale—Form 5

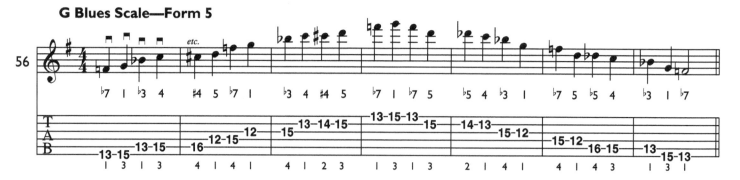

G Blues Scale
Form 5

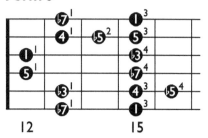

12   15

CHAPTER 13
Moving Bass

We can categorize fingerstyle pieces by what occurs on the lower strings. So far, we've played pieces with monotonic and alternating bass patterns. In this chapter, we'll look the *moving bass*. A moving bass implies a melodic line played by the thumb. Chords or phrases are then played on top of the moving bass lines; this produces two independent lines of music. It's a challenging, yet exciting style in which to play.

"Boppin' the Bass" is based on a fingerstyle *riff* (short repeated phrase) that moves from the I to the IV and V chords in the key of E.

BOPPIN' THE BASS

Track 53

All up-stem notes played with *i* & *m*;
all down-stem notes played with *p*.

Most of this next selection is based on a steady *walking bass* line. Walking bass lines are usually made of quarter notes played in patterns of whole steps and half steps. The licks on the higher strings are syncopated and give the two parts an independent sound. This is not a traditional acoustic blues style, but it's a cool way to play. Practice it slowly and work up to tempo.

Track 54

WALKIN' WITH LOU

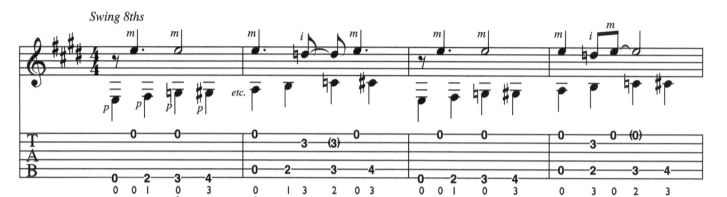

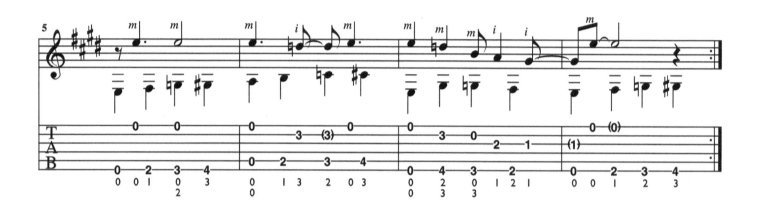

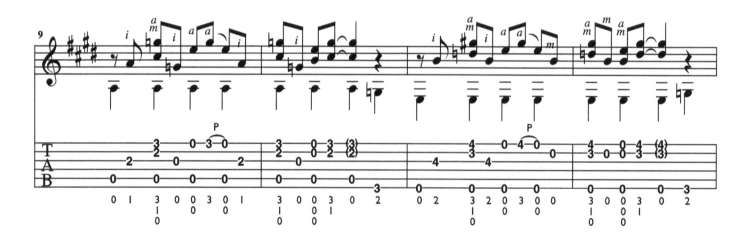

CHAPTER 14

Modes

The *modes* of the major scale are used in many styles of music. They are the basis of much early or Renaissance and Medieval music, and they are also used in many styles of ethnic and folk music. They are a vital part of jazz playing as well. Miles Davis had a significant influence by pioneering a modal approach to playing on *Kind of Blue* and other recordings. Blues players who want to go beyond the standard pentatonic and blues scales will use the *Mixolydian* and *Dorian* modes (see below) in their solos.

The term *modes* refers to a set of scales that share the same notes, but start and end from a different degree of the major scale. For example, the notes and scale degrees in a C Major scale are: C(1)–D(2)–E(3)–F(4)–G(5)–A(6)–B(7)–C(1). If we play the same notes, but start and end with D (scale degree 2), we have the D *Dorian* mode (D–E–F–G–A–B–C–D).

Each note in the major scale is the starting note of another mode. Below are all of the modes based on the C Major scale. Notice that the major scale also has a modal name—the *Ionian* mode.

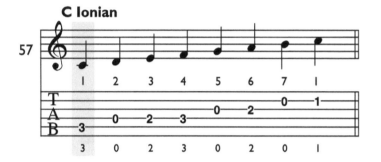

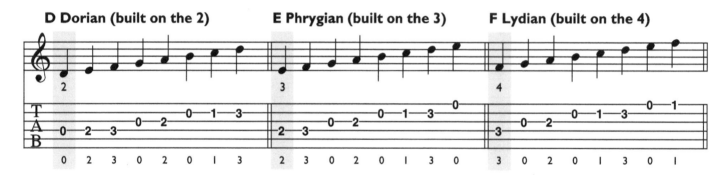

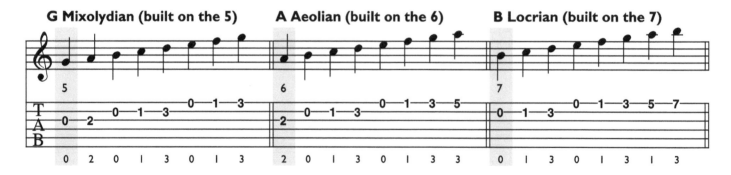

Every major scale has its own set of modes. For example, the 2 of the G Major scale is A, so the second mode of the G Major scale is A Dorian. We'll look at the Mixolydian and Dorian modes in this book because they are the two that blues players use the most. For a more in depth study of modes and their uses, check out Jody Fisher's *Guitar Mode Encyclopedia* (Alfred Music #4445).

CHAPTER 15

Mixolydian Mode

We learned that the *Mixolydian* mode is built on the 5th degree of the major scale. For example, if we want to play the A Mixolydian mode, we need to figure out *which* major scale has A as the fifth note. We can do this by finding the note that is a 5th (three-and-a-half steps) below A—that note is D. Therefore, A is the 5th degree in the D Major scale. So, to play the A Mixolydian mode, play the notes of the D Major scale starting and ending with A. This method shows us the relationship between the modes and their parent major scales, but it's a little tricky when you actually want to *play* the modes.

Another way to understand the modes is to compare them with a major scale that has the same starting note. This is called the *parallel* method. We'll use this approach to learn an A Mixolydian fingering by comparing it to an A Major scale.

A Major Scale

A Major Scale

Now let's compare the notes in the A Mixolydian Mode (A–B–C♯–D–E–F♯–G♮) to the notes in the A Major scale (A–B–C♯–D–E–F♯–G♯). They are the same except for their 7s. We can say that when compared to the major scale, the Mixolydian mode has a ♭7.

MIXOLYDIAN MODE—FORM 1

The following fingering is one of the most popular Mixolydian fingerings. Pay extra attention to the locations of the ♭7s. These are the notes that distinguish the mode and give it its unique color. Good players target, or emphasize, these notes in their solos.

A Mixolydian Mode—Form 1

A Mixolydian Mode Form 1

Another way to look at the Mixolydian mode is to see it as a major pentatonic scale with an added 6 and ♭7. If you play the above Mixolydian fingering, leaving out the 4 and ♭7, you will get the A Major Pentatonic scale.

The Mixolydian mode is a common choice in jazz or jump blues where you'll hear phrases in the style of our next example. The notes on the 3rd and 4th strings are fingered differently than the two-octave Mixolydian form we've already covered. You can choose to alter fingerings to make a phrase flow better.

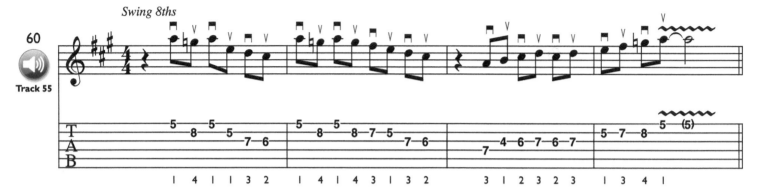

For our next example, we'll move our Mixolydian pattern from the key of A to the key of D. We'll do this by moving up the fretboard to the 10th position.

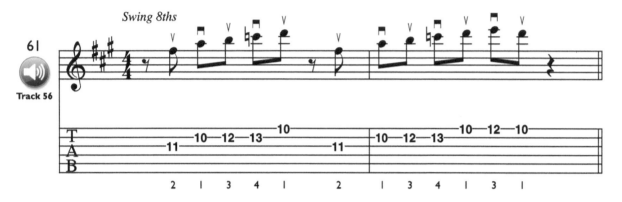

MIXOLYDIAN MODE—FORM 2

Here is another fingering for the Mixolydian mode. It's in the key of D with the tonic on the 5th string. You'll soon see why it's helpful to have more than one fingering for this mode.

D Mixolydian Mode—Form 2

**D Mixolydian Mode
Form 2**

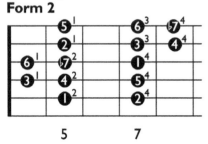

Here is a short phrase based on this new D Mixolydian fingering.

63
Track 57

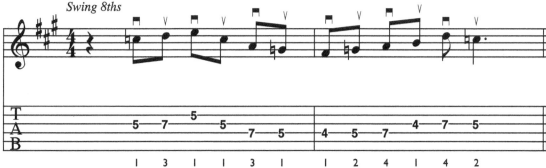

USING THE MIXOLYDIAN MODE

The Mixolydian mode is used over dominant seventh (7) chords, with the letter name of the mode matching the letter name of each chord. The chords in the following song are A7, D7 and E7. The solo moves from A to D to E Mixolydian to match the chords. We could use the same fingering for A, D and E, moving it up and down the neck, but the music will have a smoother feel if we use two fingerings and less shifting. By using Forms 1 and 2, we can stay in the same position for A and D, and we move the D fingering up two frets for E Mixolydian. Memorize this 12-bar solo and use these phrases in your own playing. On the recording, the solo is played once, then the progression is played two more times so you can practice improvising with the Mixolydian mode.

MIXING IT UP

Track 58

CHAPTER 16

Slide in Open Tunings

Before delving into this chapter, be sure you're up to date on the slide technique tips at the beginning of Chapter 11 (pages 214–215). You must have the muting techniques down to sound good playing slide in open tunings. Open G and D (and their higher equivalents of A and E) are popular slide tunings. Our first piece in open G has phrases in the style of many traditional country blues slide players. Starting with measure 13, some of the bass notes are palm muted. This is a technique where you place the pinky side of your right hand on the bridge to slightly muffle the strings as you play them.

P.M. = *Palm mute*

JAMMIN' IN G

Track 59

All single up-stem notes played with *i*
unless marked with *m*;
all double up-stemmed notes brushed up with *i*;
all down-stem notes played with *p*.

Open G Tuning

Swing 8ths

"D for Dee" is in open D tuning. It combines notes played with the slide and notes that are fretted with left-hand fingers. Bukka White and Furry Lewis, among many others, played pieces in this style.

D FOR DEE

Track 60

All 1st string notes play with *m*;
all 2nd string notes play with *i* ;
all down-stem notes play with *p*.

Open D Tuning

Swing 8ths

"Dusty Road Blues" is in the style of some of slide guitar's greatest hits. You've probably heard similar tunes played by Elmore James, Eric Clapton, Taj Mahal and many others.

DUSTY ROAD BLUES

Track 61

Use vibrato in each position;
all notes on 1st string played with *m*;
all notes on 2nd string played with *i*;
all up-stem notes played with slide (unless open string);
all down-stem notes played with *p*.

CHAPTER 17

Dorian Mode

When we looked at the Mixolydian mode in Chapter 15 (page 227), we compared it to the major scale. We saw that it is identical to the major scale except for a ♭7. When compared to the major scale with the same starting note, the Dorian mode has a ♭3 and a ♭7. So the formula for the Dorian mode is: 1–2–♭3–4–5–6–♭7. Let's take a closer look at this.

A Major Scale

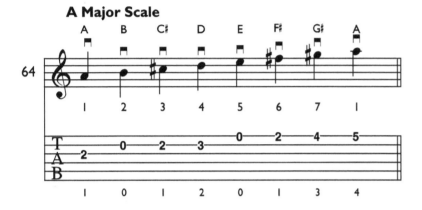

The A Dorian mode has the same notes except that a C♮ (♭3) replaces the C♯ and a G♮ (♭7) replaces the G♯.

A Dorian Mode

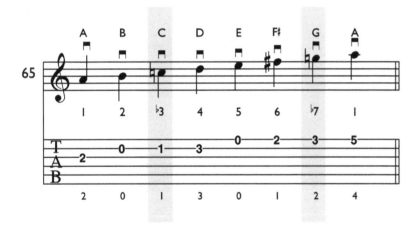

The Dorian mode has the same notes as the minor pentatonic scale, but with an added 2 and 6. Knowing this is very beneficial. If you already know the fingerings for the minor pentatonic scale, learning the Dorian mode is a snap. Just take the minor pentatonic fingerings you're comfortable with and add the 2 and 6 in each octave.

This is the most popular form of the Dorian mode. It's a movable fingering based on Form I of the minor pentatonic scale.

A Dorian Mode—Form I

A Dorian Mode
Form I

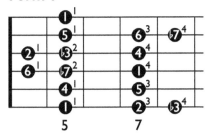

Since the 2 and 6 are notes that distinguish the Dorian mode from the minor pentatonic scale, good players target these sounds in their solos. This Dorian phrase includes these target notes and emphasizes the 2 by ending on it.

Track 62

Blues players most often use the Dorian mode to solo over minor seventh (min7) chords. Both the $\flat$3 and $\flat$7 are in both the mode and the min7 chord. The Dorian mode is also sometimes used over minor chords that are not minor sevenths.

It's important to know that the tonic of the scale needs to match the root of the chord. For example, if a blues tune starts with a Gmin7 chord, you can improvise using the G Dorian mode. If the next chord in the tune is a Cmin7, you cannot continue to improvise in G Dorian; the 6 in G Dorian would clash with the $\flat$3 in the Cmin7. So when the progression moves to Cmin7, change to a C Dorian fingering.

Most blues tunes move from a I to a IV chord. This is true in minor keys as well as major keys. When a tune moves from a imin7 to a ivmin7, we can jam over those chords with the Dorian mode that has the same tonic (or root) as the imin7 and move to the Dorian mode that has the same root as the ivmin7 chord. This is easier and will sound better if we know fingerings with tonics on the 6th and 5th strings. These two fingerings would appear in the same position on the fretboard. This can be helpful because we won't have to abruptly jump from one position to another.

DORIAN MODE—FORM 2

Here is a D Dorian fingering with its tonic on the 5th string.

D Dorian Mode—Form 2

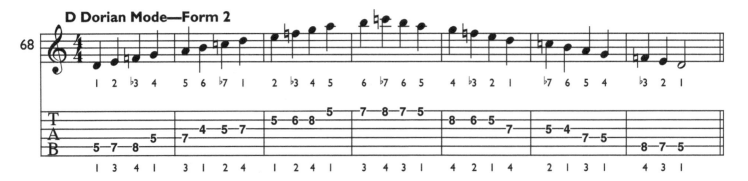

**D Dorian Mode
Form 2**

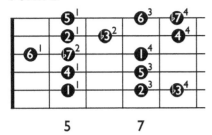

This phrase is based on the above D Dorian fingering.

Track 63

In the following solo, A Dorian is used over the Amin7 chord, and D Dorian is used over Dmin7. The chord progression is a typical minor blues. The Amin7 is the i chord and the Dmin7 is the iv. In most minor blues, the V chord is not a minor chord. It's more often a dominant 7th or a variation of a dominant 7th. In this blues, the V is a funky E7#9, and an E Minor Pentatonic scale is used to solo over it. On the recording, after the solo is played, the progression is played two more times so you can practice using these Dorian mode fingerings and licks.

DORIAN DAYS

Track 64

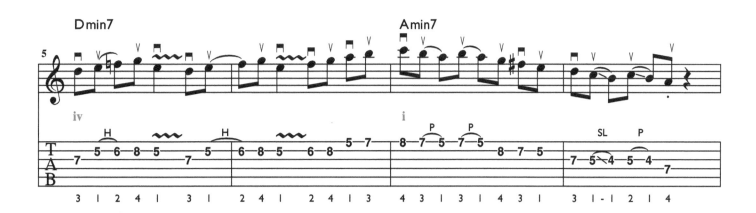

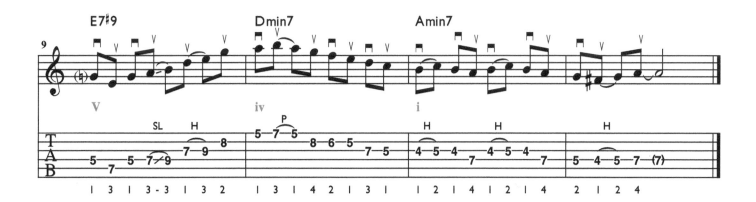

CHAPTER 18

Jazz Blues

We took our first look at jazz blues progressions on page 156. We also covered some jazzy 9th, 13th and diminished 7th chords. In this chapter, we'll move the blues even further into the jazz style. The first two pieces should be strummed with a pick or your thumb. After those, we'll do a fingerstyle jazz blues.

"Jazz Meets the Blues" is based on a popular progression. Learn it in B♭, then learn and practice it in other keys as well.

JAZZ MEETS THE BLUES

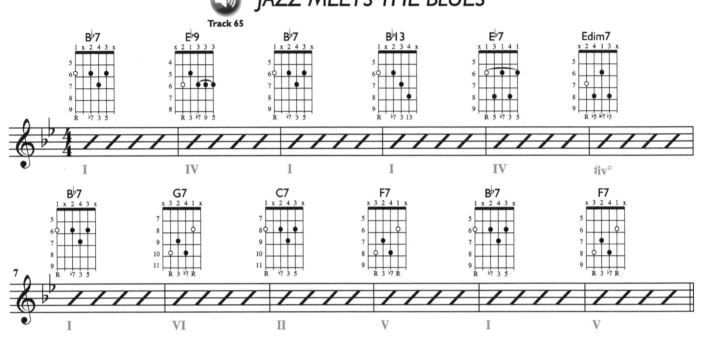

"Tune for Toots" is based on the same progression as the example above, but adds a few more chords, taking it further into the jazz realm. The fingerings for E♭13, the last B♭13 and the C9 appear here for the first time in this blues series. The C9 is interesting in that it does not have a root as a component. Jazz players quite often choose rootless fingerings because they emphasize the higher, more colorful chord tones.

TUNE FOR TOOTS

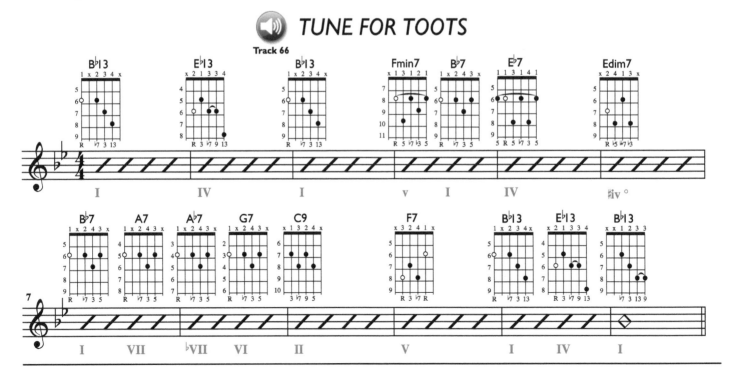

This jazzy 8-bar blues is called "Major Minor Moment" because of the D7 (IV) to Dmin7 (iv) in the 4th bar. This is a fairly common change, although not as common as a IV moving up a half step to a diminished 7th (as the IV did in our last two pieces). The Beatles also used this major/minor move in some songs. Notice the E Aug (V+) in the last measure. This is an E Augmented chord and means the 5 is raised a half step to ♯5.

MAJOR MINOR MOMENT

Track 67

CHAPTER 19

Left-Hand Muting Techniques

Muting with the left hand allows us to produce a percussive sound on the guitar. When muted strings are struck, we get an unpitched, drum-like sound that adds a unique rhythmic element and color to the music. It's a funky way to make the music sound even more exciting.

Touch the strings lightly with your left-hand fingers, but do not press them down into the fretboard, then strum or pick the strings. Muted sounds, sometimes known as *chucks*, are notated with an ×. We can use a single × even when muting multiple strings. These exercises alternate between double stops and muted strings. Play the notes clearly and then move your fingers to quickly mute the strings. Practice the example below, then tackle "Muting in A."

× = Chuck

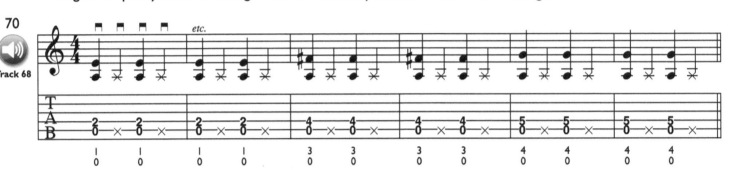

MUTING IN A

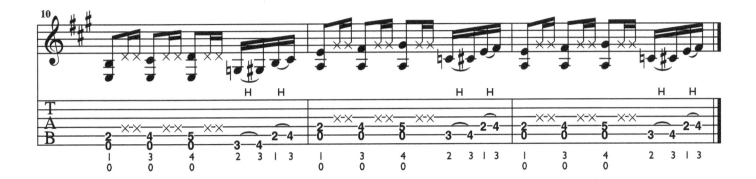

USING MUTING TECHNIQUES WHEN IMPROVISING

This technique has been used to great effect by David Bromberg in his acoustic guitar solos. The next exercise moves up the 3rd string with additional muted notes on the open 1st and 2nd strings. Picking each string with an upstroke will give the phrase a natural sound and feel. Using your first left-hand finger for all the notes will make the muting easier. The muted first two strings are notated with two × symbols on the staff and in the TAB. Be sure to listen to the recording so you know how it's supposed to sound.

32nd notes are half the value of 16th notes. Eight 32nd notes make up one beat.

The following example uses the above technique. The muted sounds add emphasis to the C that follows them.

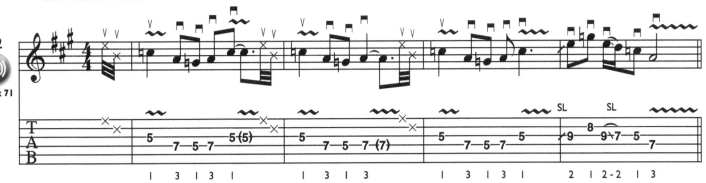

Now we're going to play some double stops in the key of B Minor. There is no muting within the phrase, but we're using this technique to fill in the space between the end of the phrase and its repeat. Muting can be a cool way to fill the space between phrases.

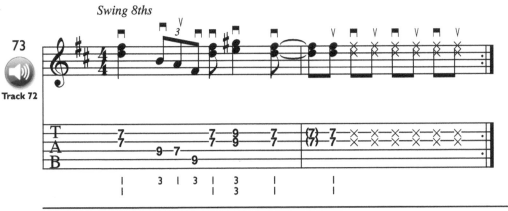

To close this chapter we'll play a riff-style blues that contains muted notes. "C Riff Blues" has muted strings strummed up and down after almost every first beat. Here, multiple strings are notated with only one ×. You won't go wrong if you aim for any set of two or three middle strings. There's no precision in muting style, you just need to keep at it until it becomes natural and sounds good.

C RIFF BLUES
Track 73

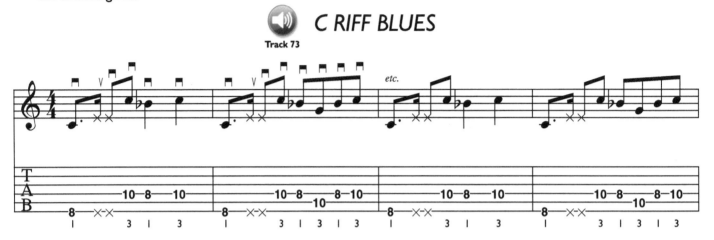

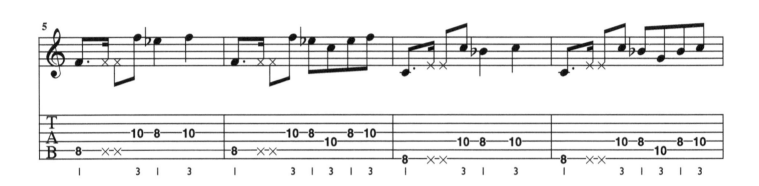

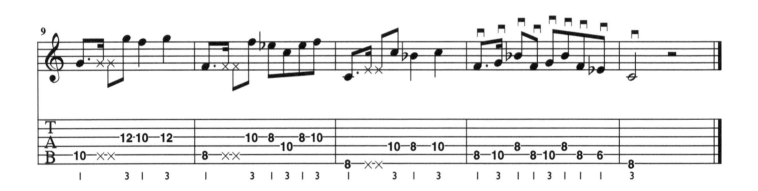

CHAPTER 20

Popping the Bass

You've heard bass players *slapping* and *popping* strings in funk styles. Guitarists have popped notes since the early days of the blues. This technique is usually used on the lower notes. Put your thumb between the string and the top of the guitar, then pull and release the string. Practice a few pops to get a feel for them.

Pops are indicated by the symbol ⌀. This symbol is taken from classical string notation where a pop is called a *Bartok pizz.* (pizz. stands for *pizzicato* which means to pluck a string).

⌀ = *Pop* or *pluck* the note.

In "Pop Goes the Bass Note," every note on the 6th string should be popped. Note the hammer-ons in measure 6. Their starting notes are grace notes which means they have no rhythmic value of their own; play the starting grace note and quickly hammer-on to the next note.

POP GOES THE BASS NOTE

Track 74

Our next piece is in open G tuning and in the style of delta bluesmen like Charley Patton and Willie Brown. The early players did not always follow the restrictions of $\frac{4}{4}$ time or the 12-bar blues form. They added and/or dropped beats and bars here and there as they felt it, letting the phrasing guide the rhythmic groupings rather than letting the rhythm guide the phrasing. "Down in the Delta" moves between $\frac{5}{4}$ and $\frac{4}{4}$ with a classic descending bass passage that is popped. Brushing the upper notes with your *i* finger will give you a rough and rugged Delta sound.

All up-stem notes are played with the *i* finger brushing up, except for the first half of the fifth beat in the $\frac{5}{4}$ bars, where *i* strums down.

All bass notes are palm muted except in the $\frac{5}{4}$ bars where they are popped.

DOWN IN THE DELTA

Track 75

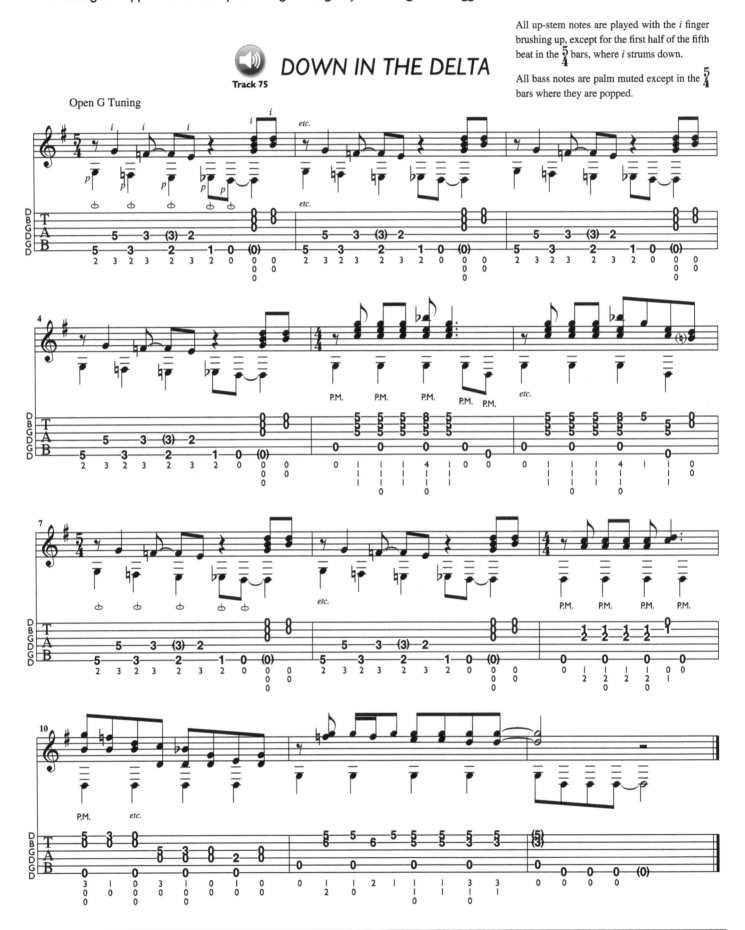

"Hot Time" starts with a great ♭3/♮3 hammer-on. It combines popping with palm muting. Palm mute all 6th string notes and pop all the notes on the 4th, 5th and 6th strings. The notes on the 6th string should have a "thumpy" sound. The other popped notes should be fairly clear. Notice the symbol > under the last notes in some of the bars. These indicate *accents,* so hit the notes below them a little more forcefully. Play it like you mean it and have fun with "Hot Time."

HOT TIME

Track 76

> = Accent

FINAL THOUGHTS

Thank you for letting me help you add more blues to your life. I hope you make the music and techniques in this book your own. Through the blues you can express all your emotions, so keep on playing and sharing those feelings with others. I'm always amazed that regardless of how much we learn there is always some really cool stuff around the corner. So keep on turning those corners and have fun along the way.

Because it's vital for you to hear the artists who created and developed the acoustic blues, there is a comprehensive list of players on page 247. Over the many years I've been playing, I've listened to all the guitarists on the list—on recordings and in live settings as well.

The musicians on this list are either exclusively acoustic players or performers who have recorded on both acoustic and electric guitars. A good library in your area may have recordings of many of these players. There are also many blues compilations that will give you a taste of various performers.

The list is divided into two categories. The Early Blues Players were members of the original wave of country blues recording artists. The Contemporary Blues Players are the more recent musicians who were influenced by the early performers and have brought acoustic blues to newer generations of listeners. Asterisks * are placed next to those in the Early Players list who are particularly important and influential. These are the *must hear* players. Howlin' Wolf did not make the list because he was a singer and electric player—but you should listen to his music as well.

If you have any questions or comments please get in touch with me at: loumanzi@snet.net.

APPENDIX

Artists

EARLY BLUES PLAYERS

Pink Anderson (1900–1974)
Barbecue Bob (1902–1931)
Scrapper Blackwell (1903–1962)
* Blind Blake (1895–1937)
Big Bill Broonzy (1893–1958)
Willie Brown (1900–1952)
Joe Calicott (1900–1969)
Bo Carter (1893–1964)
Sam Chatmon (1897–1983)
Arthur "Big Boy" Crudup (1905–1974)
* Rev. Gary Davis (1896–1972)
Sleepy John Estes (1899–1977)
Blind Boy Fuller (1908–1941)
Jesse Fuller (1896–1976)
* Lightnin' Hopkins (1912–1982)
* Son House (1902–1988)
* Mississippi John Hurt (1893–1966)
John Jackson (1924–2002)
* Skip James (1902–1969)
* Blind Lemon Jefferson (1893–1929)
* Blind Willie Johnson (1902–1947)

Lonnie Johnson (1899–1970)
* Robert Johnson (1911–1938)
Tommy Johnson (1896–1956)
* Leadbelly (1888–1949)
Furry Lewis (1893–1981)
Robert Lockwood Jr. (b. 1915)
Mississippi Fred McDowell (1904–1972)
Brownie McGhee (1915–1996)
Blind Willie McTell (1901–1959)
Memphis Jug Band (1920s–1930s)
Memphis Minnie (1897–1973)
* Charley Patton (1897–1934)
Mississippi Sheiks (late 1920s–early 1930s)
Frank Stokes (1888–1955)
Henry "Ragtime Texas" Thomas (1874–1930)
Muddy Waters (1915–1983)
Bukka White (1906–1977)
Josh White (1914–1969)
Robert Wilkins (1896–1987)
Big Joe Williams (1903–1982)
Robert Pete Williams (1914–1980)

CONTEMPORARY BLUES PLAYERS

Rory Block (b. 1949)
Roy Book Binder (b. 1941)
David Bromberg (b. 1945)
John Cephas (b. 1930)
Ry Cooder (b. 1947)
Guy Davis (b. 1952)
Paul Geremia (b. 1944)
John Hammond Jr. (b. 1942)
Corey Harris (b. 1969)
Alvin Youngblood Hart (b. 1963)
Steve James (b. 1950)
Larry Johnson (b. 1938)

Jorma Kaukonen (b. 1940)
Chris Thomas King (b. 1964)
Jim Kweskin & the Jug Band (1960s)
Taj Mahal (b. 1942)
Keb' Mo' (b. 1951)
Geoff Muldaur (b. 1945)
Bonnie Raitt (b. 1949)
Paul Rishell (b. 1950)
Chris Smither (b. 1944)
Dave Van Ronk (1936–2002)
Eric Von Schmidt (b. 1930)
Chris Whitley (1960–2005)

* Acoustic blues guitarists who were particularly important and influential.